W9-BTF-753

Frenemies in the Family

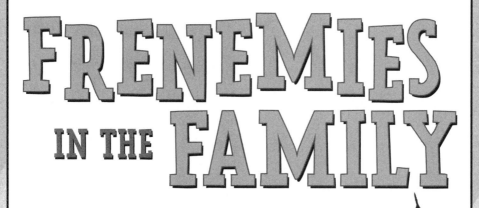

FRENEMIES
IN THE FAMILY

Famous Brothers and Sisters Who
Butted Heads and Had Each Other's Backs

Written by **Kathleen Krull**

Illustrated by **Maple Lam**

Text copyright © 2018 by Kathleen Krull
Jacket art and interior illustrations copyright © 2018 by Maple Lam

Visit us on the Web! rhcbooks.com

Educators and librarians, for a variety of teaching tools, visit us at RHTeachersLibrarians.com

Library of Congress Cataloging-in-Publication Data
Names: Krull, Kathleen, author. | Lam, Maple, illustrator.
Title: Frenemies in the family : famous brothers and sisters who butted heads
and had each other's backs / Kathleen Krull ; illustrated by Maple Lam.
Other titles: Famous brothers and sisters who butted heads and had each other's backs
Description: First edition. | New York : Crown Books for Young Readers, [2018] |
Audience: Grades 4–6. | Audience: Ages 8–12.
Identifiers: LCCN 2017038405 | ISBN 978-0-399-55124-6 (hardcover) |
ISBN 978-0-399-55126-0 (epub) | ISBN 978-0-399-55125-3 (glb)
Subjects: LCSH: Brothers and sisters—Case studies—Juvenile literature. | Sibling rivalry—
Juvenile literature. | Brothers and sisters—United States—Biography—Juvenile literature.
Classification: LCC BF723.S43 K78 2018 | DDC 306.875—dc23

Printed in the United States of America
10 9 8 7 6 5 4 3 2 1
First Edition

To the Secret Garage Club—
Ken, Carleton, and Kevin, my brothers

Contents

Introduction

Siblings! You can't live with them; you can't launch them into space.

Revelry, rivalry, a rumpus of emotions, whipped into a froth of teeth gnashing and hair tearing.

Unless you're an only child (oh, boo-hoo), who *doesn't* have a juicy sibling story?

Even famous people do—read on. In chronological order, meet siblings who were BFFs, deeply attached, or even literally attached.

And meet others who were candidates for the Bad Sibling Hall of Fame, in cutthroat competition, or even homicidal.

Sometimes siblings band together against cruel parents—or against the cruel world. More often, though, they butt heads. Oh, brother! Oh, sister!

So, next time you:

—get blamed for something your sibling did,

—have hand-to-hand combat about who sits in the front seat of the car,

—find rude comments scribbled by a sibling in your private diary,

—have to share a room with a sibling with personal habits the opposite of yours,

  —lose the race to get to the shower first in the morning,

  —have to listen to a sibling's wretched taste in music,

  —reach for the last cupcake and it's gone,

  —or any of a million other sibling devilries . . .

instead of screaming, savor these stories and try to look forward to celebrating National Siblings Day next April 10.

Queens Elizabeth I & Mary I (Bloody Mary)

Your Sister Wants
to Kill You—Really

The British king Henry VIII doted on his daughter Mary—at first. "This girl never cries!" he boasted.

In 1520, at four years old, Princess Mary was entertaining foreign visitors with her performances on the harpsichord. By nine, she could read and write Latin. Her mother, Catherine of Aragon, oversaw her education, and Henry approved, calling Mary his "pearl of the world" and "token of hope"—even though, like pretty much every king, what he really wanted was a son.

Poor Mary!

Her dad was without question one of the world's worst husbands, with six wives in all. Henry VIII left the Catholic faith (and forced all his subjects to join him) so that he could divorce Catherine on shaky grounds (mainly that lack-of-a-son thing) and banish her from court. It was a terrible blow to seventeen-year-old Mary, who never saw her mother again.

Even worse, Henry's next wife, Anne Boleyn, had a daughter, Elizabeth, who instantly became the Favored One. Anne stripped Mary of her princess title and forced her to act as lady-in-waiting to the new princess, her baby half sister.

The indignities piled up. Mary actually had to walk *behind* the baby—sometimes it took slaps to enforce this. Elizabeth got the

place of honor at the table (Mary ate in her rooms). The baby was dressed in gold-embroidered caps, gowns of green satin or orange velvet. No expense was spared for her, while Mary had to give up servants and return some of her jewels. When Mary protested, Henry dispatched his most important duke—who threatened to crack her skull against the wall.

Perhaps Mary never cried as a baby, but now that was all she did, presumably out of her dad's hearing.

Poor Elizabeth!

Before she reached her third birthday, Henry had Anne beheaded (yes, one of the reasons: Elizabeth wasn't a son). Elizabeth is known to have mentioned Anne only twice afterward but all her life treasured a ring with two miniature portraits of her and her mom.

Poor sisters!

After Henry's *next* marriage, the sisters had a half brother, Edward, the new Favored One. His mother, Jane Seymour, died two weeks after his birth (before Henry thought of a reason to dispose of her). The two girls were pushed aside while Edward was groomed to be the next ruler.

By age six, Elizabeth was noted for her unsmiling face; people said that she looked as serious as a forty-year-old. Her dad's main interest was her moral development, and his theory of child rearing involved surrounding her with "ancient and sad persons."

She was rescued by a stepmom, the king's sixth and final

wife. Unusually well educated for her day, Catherine Parr made a point of seeing that the obviously promising Elizabeth got the same rigorous education given to male heirs—languages, history, rhetoric, and philosophy. Usually, education for women was sketchy, as you can tell from her tutor's compliments: "Her mind has no womanly weakness," he wrote; "her perseverance is equal to that of a man, and her memory long keeps what it quickly picks up."

Elizabeth ended up much better educated than Mary, who was understandably bitter and insecure. Her father was too busy with his own marriages to arrange one for Mary. At twenty-five, she had no real role—she was just "Lady Mary, and the most unhappy lady in Christendom."

Elizabeth was thirteen when Henry died. She grieved briefly but immediately regained her famous composure. Mostly he had scared her.

Since women had no power of their own, even nine-year-old Edward was seen as the better choice to rule than his older sisters. When he became king, the men around him began jockeying to be the power behind the throne. Mary and Elizabeth were pawns, tense rivals at a time when everyone around them was plotting for their own gain. People watched closely to see which sister was in favor, and the sisters simply avoided each other during his reign.

When Edward caught an infection and died at age fifteen, in 1553, Mary saw her chance and proclaimed herself England's first ruling queen. Elizabeth immediately wrote to congratulate her. Then Mary rode triumphantly into London, with Elizabeth riding right behind her, careful not to attract *too* much attention but also wanting their people to see her at her best.

The show of sisterly love was just that—a show. Mary began making her mistrust very clear. Enemies *were* conspiring against her, and Elizabeth had no real way to prove she wasn't one of them.

Perfecting the art of the "answerless answer," Elizabeth lived in constant dread, her expression usually one of alarm.

No one knew quite what to do with her: Keep her close? Send her away? Anything she did could give Mary a reason to execute her, and Mary really wanted to, but . . . Elizabeth had many supporters. Plus, she was her *sister.*

So Mary played mind games. When Elizabeth would ask to see her, Mary would make her wait days in suspense before answering. Some days they sat together at meals and Mary gave her fur coats or jewels; other days Elizabeth was kept isolated. It was obvious that Mary wanted to keep tabs on her, but really, she couldn't stand to be around her younger sister.

Elizabeth felt humiliated, which was sort of the point.

Queen Mary was unpopular from the get-go. She was Catholic in a mainly Protestant country, and she had no talent for politics.

And she was a woman in charge, which was frowned upon at the time. A famous preacher wrote his disapproval: "It is more than a monster in nature that a woman should reign and bear empire above man."

Mary's unpopularity only increased when, at thirty-seven, she married another Catholic, King Philip II of Spain, and set about restoring England to its original faith, by force when necessary. She revived the laws against heresy (violations of religious laws) and started torturing and killing Protestant heretics, displaying the rotting corpses all around London as warnings.

Now you know why she was called Bloody Mary. During her five-year reign, she had over 280 heretics burned at the stake. Crowds would gather, munching on snacks, to watch the gory spectacle.

Her violent persecution didn't go over well, and people began to look at Elizabeth as a better option. Sure, she was a woman too, but at least she was a staunch Protestant. It was only a matter of time before this Draft Elizabeth campaign got her into trouble and she was brought to court for questioning.

At age twenty, though fervently claiming her innocence, Elizabeth was ordered by Mary to be imprisoned for treason in

the Tower of London. On the way there, she staged one of the first sit-ins and had to be carried inside. The next two months were mental torture—no books, pure boredom, no visitors, no news. She was left to think about things such as how to persuade her captors to bring in an executioner from France, because they did a cleaner job. . . .

Mary did not mess around. After this plot, she executed the leader (and also had him drawn and quartered), plus a hundred of his followers, as well as her cousin Jane, also a rival for the throne.

But after extensive interrogation and spying had revealed no hard evidence of treason on her part, Elizabeth did get released from the Tower. Her release was probably thanks to Philip. If Mary died and Elizabeth wasn't around, the English crown might go to their cousin Mary, Queen of Scots, creating a French alliance that Philip, the Spanish king as well as Mary's husband, considered disastrous. What a twisted family tree they had.

For the rest of her life, Elizabeth shuddered when she had to visit the Tower or even pass by it.

Just because Mary spared Elizabeth's life didn't mean she trusted her. She placed her sister under house arrest in a private home for almost a year. The conditions were better than in the Tower, but she had little to occupy her mind besides exchanging angry letters with Mary, which only made matters worse.

Mary's biggest nightmare was for Elizabeth to get the crown. It was unthinkable that a Protestant would follow her on the throne. So she was desperate to have a child who would be her heir.

In an era when much about childbirth was mysterious, she had symptoms of pregnancy but never actually had a baby. It seemed to be a case of recurring false pregnancy.

For her very survival, Elizabeth had to pretend to go along with Mary's policies. But the sisters were still playing mind games, and Mary could see through Elizabeth's lies.

In 1558, Elizabeth was called to court to attend the final stages of Mary's latest apparent pregnancy. Mary wanted to lord it over her—if she gave birth to a healthy child, Elizabeth's chances of becoming queen went way down. But again there was no child. In fact, instead of bringing a new life into the world, Mary, at age forty-two, was actually dying, possibly of cancer.

After her sister *promised* to keep pushing to make England Catholic, Mary finally named Elizabeth her heir.

Elizabeth, now gloriously free of siblings, came to the throne amid bells, bonfires, and all sorts of gleeful demonstrations.

But many still thought women were unfit to govern, and Mary's reign hadn't done much to correct the impression.

Elizabeth had to chart her own path—and that included tolerance of all religions. She immediately reneged on her deathbed promise to Mary, stopped the executions, and released all Protestants from prison. The whole country sighed with relief. Maybe a woman *could* rule.

Mary had actually made the concept easier to accept. She paved the way, and Elizabeth was able to learn from her mistakes. She was charismatic and a superb politician, always pragmatic. People liked her. They thought of her as a sort of honorary man, and she tried to present herself that way, as her father Henry's replacement. Like him, she had a spectacular temper, complete with swearing, spitting, screaming, slapping, bullying, death threats—which she sometimes carried out. Mostly the atmosphere in her court was one of fun, wit, and romance. Should anyone displease her, though, the air would suddenly chill.

When her ladies-in-waiting played

tricks on her and showed disrespect, she broke the finger of one and stabbed another in the hand with a fork. When an obscene pamphlet about her appeared, she had its author and his publisher arrested and their right hands chopped off. When her favorite companion started a rebellion, she had him executed. She never married, having seen only bad marriages around her—and also dreading a husband's interference with her rule. During her sibling-free reign—over the next forty-four years—England became a major player on the world stage in politics, business, and the arts. She provided much-needed stability for the kingdom and helped forge a sense of national identity. Most of all, her religious toler- ance meant a lack of holy wars, which were wrecking other countries.

It was Elizabeth who had the last laugh and gave her name to the whole era: the Elizabethan Age.

When Your *Cousin* Wants to Kill You

Elizabeth actually did execute a relative. Her closest heir was her cousin Mary, Queen of Scots.

Also known as Mary Stuart, she was a Catholic supported by powerful Catholic countries such as France. Protestants had déjà vu—Bloody Mary all over again.

It was too dangerous to let Mary leave England to go back to Scotland, but Elizabeth didn't know what to do except keep her imprisoned. Mary didn't help herself by constantly plotting against Elizabeth.

After an especially blatant conspiracy to murder her in 1587, Elizabeth dithered for three months—and then with great reluctance had her cousin beheaded.

Bloody Mary executed over 280 people for heresy, more than any other English ruler. But she wasn't the only royal who killed people.

By comparison, her father, Henry, executed as many as 70,000 people, for all kinds of reasons.

Half sister Elizabeth had 200 Catholics hanged. Mary's grandparents Ferdinand and Isabella burned 2,000 Muslims, Jews, and Protestants during the Spanish Inquisition.

But, perhaps unfairly, it was Mary who got stuck with the name.

A New Word: "Siblicide"

Killing your siblings is rare among humans. It's frowned upon and has penalties. It's more likely to occur in the animal world.

Black-widow spider babies eat their weaker brothers and sisters, and some two dozen species of birds do away with theirs.

Why? Life in the animal world can be harsh when food sources dwindle.

Eliminating your competition means more for you, and you're more likely to survive and pass on your genes.

Sibling Rivalry

This term, meaning competition (sometimes bitter) for attention from your parents, wasn't coined until 1941—four hundred years after these Tudor sisters. But don't you think Elizabeth and Bloody Mary are the perfect example?

Chang & Eng Bunker

"We Had to Get Along"

Imagine that you had a brother or sister attached to you. Like, literally. Another person at your side every second of every minute of every day. Sure, you'd never be lonely. But would it not also be very, very irritating?

Chang and Eng, known as the Siamese twins because of their birthplace, in Siam, were in this very pickle. They were twins, but not the usual sort of twins. Their two complete bodies were joined at the base of their chests by a thick band of flesh. They were conjoined—permanently. Face to face, and then, as they learned to stretch the band slightly, side by side.

Always, always, always. Peeing, pooping, sleeping, doing

everything that humans do. For sixty-two years, with never a moment's privacy.

Their lives began in 1811 near Bangkok, in the isolated Kingdom of Siam, later known as Thailand. The "double boys" were a magnet for attention. Doctors itched to separate them with crude tools like a saw or a burning wire, or to stretch them apart in various unpleasant ways. Their mother refused. Such methods would kill one or both. She wasn't willing to lose either of them. For their own sibling survivalry, the boys belonged together.

They grew up poor, along a river in a village of floating houses. Learning to walk was a more intense struggle for them than for most children. The brothers had to master the coordination of their muscles, then work together fiercely to become agile.

In time they learned to swim, and their father taught them acrobatic moves. By the time he died, the eight-year-old twins were getting around fine, raising ducks and selling their eggs to support their large family.

It was while the brothers, then fourteen, were playing together in the river that they were spotted by a British merchant. He traded in fine fabrics, opium, weapons, and medicines. When he saw the twins, he thought, *How bizarre, how unique . . . how great an opportunity. Think of the money they could bring in if they were exhibited to audiences.*

Their mother needed convincing—some sort of payment was made to her, some sort of contract signed—and it took a long time to get the king's permission for his subjects to leave the country.

And then, one day, Chang and Eng sailed west, hungry for adventure and, with the promise of future riches, proud to be helping their family. On board the ship was a translator, and the twins picked up English quickly. Little did they realize they would never see their mother or any of their family again.

It was going to be the two of them alone, together.

The merchant teamed up with an American sea captain to manage the brothers and put them on stage in theaters and concert halls across America and England. You could see the "Siamese twins" from exotic Siam, a country almost unknown to the West, for fifty cents a person.

At their first show, in Boston, Chang and Eng didn't exactly perform. They simply stood on stage, demonstrated how they walked and ran, and answered questions. But they kept adding more to their act—somersaults, backflips, walking on their hands, and shows of strength, like lifting up the heaviest audience member. Though the two weighed only 180 pounds when they started on stage, over time they bulked up and became ever stronger.

They added a badminton-like game, batting at each other across a specially designed net. They mastered chess, playing against each other or with people in the audience. They also engaged in clever wordplay.

Astounding! The twins were a sensation, a genuine human mystery. Over the years they were seen by more people around the world than any other entertainers of the day.

Everyone gasped at how they could move in unison, two acting as one.

How did they *do* it? It seemed that Chang and Eng had perfected the art of compromise, cooperation, negotiation. They excelled at "reading" each other. More than any siblings in history, perhaps, they simply got along. They reveled in being together.

Naturally, doctors wanted to examine them. The twins were patient about it, up to a point.

One doctor had Chang eat asparagus, finding out that his urine had the distinct asparagus smell, while Eng's did not. But one's toothache kept the other awake. And when one was tickled, the other would complain, telling the doctor to cut it out. When strong pressure was applied to the band, the twins would faint.

Even as they slept—some nine to eleven hours a night—the brothers were under inspection. If they wanted to change position, a newspaper reported, "the one must roll entirely over the

20

other; they have been frequently observed to do this without either waking or being apparently disturbed by the change."

The brothers tried to be charming and good humored, though rude or stupid questions made them twitch. To be addressed as "boys" when they were actually young men clearly annoyed them. Being called liars or frauds really made them mad. They were dignified and wanted to be treated that way.

They shared tastes and opinions to an amazing degree. Sometimes they said the same thing at the same time. Some observers even speculated that they could read each other's minds.

Toward each other they were usually loving and tender. They would pat each other's cheek or adjust a shirt collar when necessary. When one wanted privacy, the other had an uncanny ability to tune out and leave him be.

Doctors constantly proposed ways to separate the twins and give them "normal" lives. Most deemed surgery far too risky. Anyway, the brothers showed little interest. Just talking about it upset them.

Over three years, the managers drove the twins at a challenging pace. The brothers grew weary; plus, they could see they were not always being treated fairly.

At age twenty-one they declared independence. To celebrate, they bought and gave away five hundred cigars.

They kept touring another seven years, in charge of their own finances and saving up. Their work ethic was stellar—they never slacked off.

The people they encountered most on a regular basis were

doctors, and one day a doctor from North Carolina talked them into a vacation there.

North Carolina had lovely forests, lots of animals to hunt, rivers jumping with trout, fertile land. A secluded, rural life here sounded tempting to the brothers. They chose to settle in a small town set against the dramatic beauty of the Blue Ridge Mountains.

It seemed like an odd choice. Few immigrants and *no* other Asians lived in the area. But the doctors they knew paved the way for them to meet lawyers and other respectable folks.

They took up farming, accumulating some thousand acres—an actual plantation. They grew crops—sweet potatoes, corn, oats, wheat—and raised cattle and sheep and pigs.

They built their own elegant house and ordered fine furniture, china, and the best silverware—knives *and* forks, not just the usual spoons. They were good hosts, keeping up with current events as the Civil War loomed.

No one protested when they applied for and received American citizenship, adopting the last name Bunker. This was a privilege limited to free white men, but the brothers just took it for granted and somehow slipped in under the radar. They were now definitely the most well-known Asian Americans of the nineteenth century, and perhaps their fame had smoothed their path.

How did they manage all the labor of running their plantation? Physically fit and working so well as a team, the twins did a lot themselves—chopping wood, building structures. But, like other landowners in the South, they also depended on slave labor.

The Bunkers ended up with so much land and so many slaves that they were among the district's wealthiest families.

Our brothers had traveled the world and made money, and were more free than most people. They were crafting a life that seemed to them ideal.

Except for one item.

Both had always counted on marrying and having children. It wasn't that they wanted more than just the two of them—they simply wanted what others had.

When they met the Yates sisters, blond teens who lived down the road, Chang decided it was time. Over years of dropping by for dinner, he wooed Adelaide Yates. Eng actually liked Adelaide too but willingly settled for her sister Sarah. They ordered a special bed built for four. There is no record of what the sisters or their family thought about any of this.

In an understatement, a newspaper called it a "Marriage Extraordinary." But again there was surprisingly little fuss. Any objections were more over the mixing of two races, strictly illegal at the time, than the brothers' unusual physique. Some people thought the marriages were a hoax, a publicity stunt for the famous pair.

They weren't faking. . . . Not quite a year later, Sarah delivered a baby girl, with Adelaide giving birth to another girl six days later. Two more babies were born the following year—and then more and more.

The twins really liked kids. Together, they had a total of twenty-one. They built a schoolhouse right on the plantation and hired a teacher. At a time when one in four children failed to reach age five, the Bunker children were comparatively healthy. Just two died as babies, and two were deaf (none were twins).

The twins still got along pretty well. The foursome—not so much. This was the only time the twins expressed a real interest in separation surgery, perhaps prompted by their wives.

Always expert at cooperation, Chang and Eng devised a less risky solution. They built separate houses a mile apart. They stuck to a schedule of three and a half days in one house with one family, then three and a half days in the other. The "guest" brother had to keep silent and go along with whatever the "host" wanted.

True, it was weird, but it worked.

During the Civil War, the famous twins were often used by newspapers as a symbol for the country—united they stand, divided they die.

But in fact they were dedicated to the Confederate cause. Two of their sons fought for the South; one was wounded, and the other was taken prisoner.

Their side, of course, lost. Losing the labor of their slaves was a blow to their finances. Time to go on tour once again: "The ravages of civil war have swept away our fortunes, and we are again forced to appear in public," they announced. To some, the twins were starting to look tacky, a bit greedy. They weren't getting much sympathy—especially in the North. So they toured abroad.

At age fifty-eight, on the way back from Germany and Russia, Chang suffered a stroke. He grew frail. He had been drinking heavily for some time and had a bad case of bronchitis.

Eng, seemingly okay, did his best to take care of him and keep up his spirits.

In 1874, at age sixty-two, Chang died in his sleep at home, probably from a blood clot. It is impossible to imagine Eng's emotion when he woke up and saw his twin brother dead beside him. But he knew what was next, reportedly announcing, "Then I am going."

For the first time in his life, Eng was alone. But after sixty-two years of such intense togetherness, solitude may have seemed unbearable. He moved his body closer to Chang's—and waited.

By the time the doctor arrived, Eng too was dead. At the time, the cause was chalked up to his shock at suddenly being alone.

Had they been born today, the twins would have easily been separated—and probably lost to history.

Together, they remain of eternal interest—unusually important brothers.

Two in One

The term "Siamese twins" is no longer used. We now know that such births can occur anywhere in the world and have done so since the beginning of history.

Today we call them conjoined twins—siblings physically joined at some point on their bodies. They are always identical twins, always the same sex.

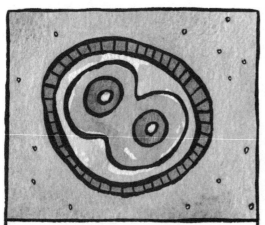

Most scientists believe that conjoined twins develop from a single fertilized egg that fails to separate completely as it divides. It's rare. Approximately two hundred pairs of conjoined twins are born alive each year.

Today it is very unusual to see them—with advances in medicine, doctors try to surgically separate them. About 75 percent of separations result in at least one twin surviving.

The king of Siam ordered their execution at birth, fearing they would bring bad luck to the country. When their mother refused to abandon them, the king eventually gave up on the death sentence.

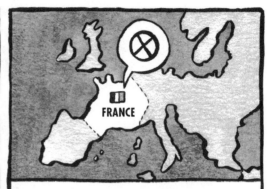

France refused to let the twins enter the country on the grounds that pregnant women who saw them might give birth to babies with deformities.

As some of the first Asians in America, the twins faced surprisingly little prejudice, but the tide was beginning to turn. When many Chinese people immigrated during the gold rush of 1848, anti-Chinese racism grew deadly, especially in the West.

By 1882, Congress banned immigration from China—the first time people were barred from America because of their race.

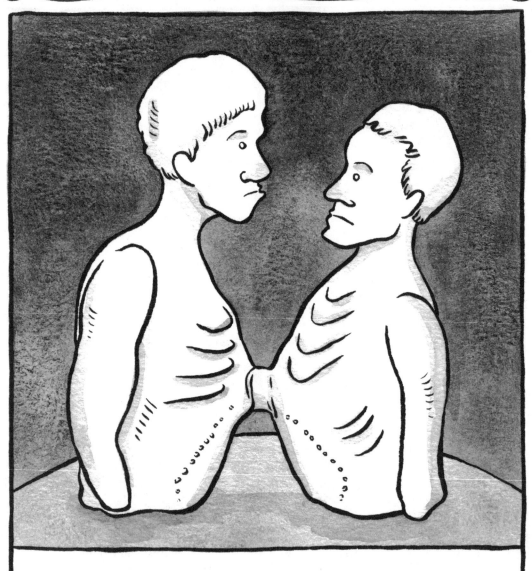

In their will, Chang and Eng expressed the wish that their bodies not be separated. Today you can view a plaster cast of their torsos at the Mütter Museum, in Philadelphia.

A Sibling Dynasty

With so many children, Chang and Eng have an unusual number of descendants—1,500.

They include eleven sets of twins, none of them conjoined.

Some get along, and some have stopped speaking to each other—just as in any other batch of siblings.

But one (a great-great-grandson) did shoot and kill his twin brother in 2003, for hiding his supply of beer.

Edwin & John Wilkes Booth

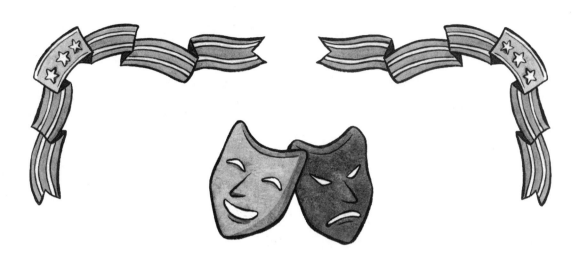

"I Have No Brother"

E dwin and John Wilkes Booth are eternally fascinating. They're perhaps the ultimate example of the good brother/ bad brother mystery. What *happens* to brothers to make them so different?

Edwin may not have always been "good." But he was an angel compared to his younger brother John, who committed one of the most horrible crimes in history—the first assassination of an American president.

Born less than five years apart, the two Booths were both famous actors, but with different careers, different personalities, and, of course, different ends.

Certainly their childhoods couldn't have been more unlike. In fact, Edwin often said he never *had* a childhood. At thirteen, he was sent on the road as a caretaker for their father, also a famous actor, but an eccentric alcoholic. Edwin had to be the parent. He had a hard life, growing up on the road, sending money home for his brothers' schooling. Off stage, he hardly smiled, brooding, haunted.

John, meanwhile, was spoiled rotten by his mother and the rest of his large family on their farm in Maryland. He was the favorite of their parents, always the center of attention—"his mother's darling," said Edwin. John was peppy, telling his sister that "life is so short, and the world is so beautiful. Just to *breathe* is delicious."

John shot cats for sport (perhaps a clue to his murderous instincts), partied hard, skipped school, and played pranks. His father refused to own slaves and instead paid workers to keep the farm going. But John made friends among the wealthy slaveholding families in Maryland, a tricky line to walk as the Civil War took shape. Maryland was a slave state but also a border state, with many who supported the North.

Between the two brothers, their father's precious costumes, carefully stored in a trunk, were a bone of contention. John once tattled on Edwin for "borrowing" a costume of Dad's—earning Edwin a beating. Later, when Edwin needed costumes, he raided Dad's trunk. His mother caught him and wouldn't let him have any—much to Edwin's annoyance, she said she was saving them all for John.

Edwin did rise above such matters, forging a distinguished career that lasted almost fifty years. Some considered him the greatest American actor of his time, and he was especially loved for his Shakespearean performances. He made the nineteenth-century equivalent of millions of dollars a year, touring America and the major capitals of Europe. In America, he stopped making appearances in the South due to his strong antislavery beliefs. He made New York his home base and founded Booth's Theatre, a spectacular venue.

Back on the farm, John was anxious to outperform his big brother. He began training his voice daily in the woods, studying Shakespeare, and drawing patrons into bars with his fierce rendition of Edgar Allan Poe's "The Raven."

At age seventeen, John made his stage debut. At first he flubbed lines while the audience hissed. One opening night, he was supposed to introduce himself by saying, "Madame, I am Petruchio Pandolfo." Instead he stammered, "Madame, I am Pondolfio Pet—Pedolfio Pat—Pantuchio Ped . . . Who am I?" The audience convulsed with laughter.

Once, he was accidentally shot in the butt by his manager while they were goofing around, just before he went on stage. It took him months to recover, but eventually his career went on.

John's performances may not have been as precise as Edwin's; they had completely different styles. But he was kind of a drama king and made up for that lack of precision with his energy. He hurled himself so strenuously around the stage that he often got hurt. Even when obviously cut and bleeding, he always finished the play. He was reported to cover himself in steaks and raw oysters while he slept, to heal his bruises. His favorite role was Brutus—the assassin of a tyrant.

John was the first actor known to have fans rip off his clothes. His striking appearance mesmerized women.

36

Each day he received fan mail from women in love with him; he had stalkers, and within five years he was earning huge sums of money. Poet Walt Whitman reported that he "would have flashes, passages, I thought, of real genius." Another critic wrote, "Without having Edwin's culture and grace, Mr. Booth has far more action, more life, and, we are inclined to think, more natural genius."

Two brothers in the same highly competitive profession— was there rivalry? Of *course* . . . John, especially, seemed irritated at brotherly comparisons. He even had a billboard printed with a pointed Shakespeare quote: "I have no brother. I am like no brother. . . . I AM MYSELF ALONE."

For his part, Edwin once wrote, with a bit of snark, "I don't think John will startle the world. But he is improving fast and looks beautiful on stage."

But the two were brought up to be Southern gentlemen, and, after all, they were actors: they knew how to *act* fond of each other.

Few were more passionate fans of the theater than President Abraham Lincoln and his wife, Mary. Escaping to plays when they could, they saw just about everyone perform, including both Booths. Lincoln enjoyed John's performances so much that he once asked to meet him after a play.

John, of course, declined. He despised everything about Lincoln—his jokes, his appearance, and, most of all, his politics.

Thoroughly racist, he raged against the president and blamed him for the war and all of the South's woes.

The Booth family, like many Maryland families, was split. As the Civil War broke out, John was gung ho for the South to secede from the Union. He argued more and more with Edwin, who favored the North. Once, they fought so bitterly that Edwin told him he was no longer welcome at his New York home.

With Lincoln's landslide reelection in 1864, John was appalled—his platform promised to abolish slavery altogether. John went berserk and started plotting against him, working with other Southern sympathizers.

In one of his last letters, he wrote that the institution of "African slavery is one of the greatest blessings that God has ever bestowed upon a favored nation." He believed that "this country was formed for the WHITE and not for the black man." Blacks, he argued, were better off under slavery, protected in a sort of father-son way. He even had the nerve to call himself a slave for being unable to speak his thoughts in Union states and his own house.

John was spinning out of control. He formed a bizarre plan to kidnap the president and hold him hostage. It came to nothing.

Then, one night in April 1865, John was in the crowd when Lincoln gave a short speech from his White House window. When Lincoln mentioned granting voting rights to the former slaves, John exploded, vowing that this would be the last speech Lincoln would ever make.

That Friday night, while Edwin was brilliantly emoting on stage at another theater, John quietly entered through a rear door at Ford's Theatre. He crept into the Lincolns' private box and shot the president in the back of the head.

Then he leaped onto the stage, brandishing a knife and—in best drama-king fashion—screamed the words of Brutus: *"Sic semper tyrannis!"* Or, in English, "Thus always to tyrants!" Crashing to the floor, he broke a bone in his left leg, but in the chaos he was able to flee on horseback.

The shocking assassination of the president of the United States spurred a giant manhunt. Even so, John survived for twelve days.

He was finally surrounded in a burning barn, where he'd been hiding. Forced out by the flames, he was shot dead at twenty-six. In his pockets were found a compass, a candle, and pictures of five girlfriends. In his last diary entry, he rambled, "For my country I have given up all that makes life sweet and holy, brought misery upon my family."

He got the last part right. The whole Booth family was immediately and quite falsely suspected of helping John. At the first reports that a crazy man named Booth had shot the president, some assumed it was Edwin. In the hysteria, most Booth siblings were placed under temporary house arrest or actually imprisoned for weeks. Headlines blared MONSTER . . . MADMAN . . . SAVAGE BEAST . . . AGENT OF THE DEVIL.

John's terrible deed shattered his family. One sister simply moved to England to escape the shame.

When Edwin first heard the news, he said, "It was just as if I have been struck in the head by a hammer." He didn't leave his apartment for months. His fiancée broke off their engagement. Friends worried he'd commit suicide and took turns staying with him.

He took out newspaper advertisements to declare that his family had *nothing* to do with "this foul and most atrocious of

crimes." He insisted that "I cannot understand why my brother did this."

Somehow, the show went on. A year later, Edwin needed money and returned to the stage. He performed for another twenty-five years. Because of constant death threats, he never took solo curtain calls, and hired someone to impersonate him at train stops.

Talk about sibling notoriety. Edwin tried to distance himself as best he could: "We regarded him as a good-hearted, harmless, though wild-brained, boy, and used to laugh at his patriotic froth whenever secession was discussed. . . . All his theatrical friends speak of him as a poor crazy boy, and such his family think of him."

Edwin was the one trying to say, *I have no brother.* As he told his sister, "Think no more of him as your brother; he is dead to us now." For the rest of his life, he tried never to speak his name again. Once, when he slipped, he burst out crying.

Ever more brooding and haunted, Edwin died at age fifty-nine after a stroke.

Good brother, bad brother—it remains a mystery.

Why Do Siblings Differ?

Some say we shape our identities in relation to our siblings, trying to develop a contrasting identity to lessen the painful rivalry. Also, studies say that each child's experience within a family can be so different (depending on birth order, gender, changing parental attitudes and circumstances, and other factors), you could say that each grows up almost in a different family.

Besides birth order, siblings get shaped by friends, teachers, even chance. One scientist has compared siblings to phone numbers—containing the same digits but arranged in different sequences.

Playing Favorites

For most of human history, blatant favoritism used to be completely acceptable. It was okay for parents to show that they liked one child more than the others. Often—but not always—it was the oldest son. It's a modern concept that this unfair treatment is cruel.

After people started talking about sibling rivalry in the 1940s, experts warned parents to treat their children equally, that playing favorites would heighten the rivalry to an unhealthy degree, setting the stage for lifelong strife.

The Good Brother Rescues Another Lincoln

Once, Abraham Lincoln's oldest son, Robert, was traveling by train, getting scrunched on a crowded platform.

Off balance, he fell into the space between the platform and the train. A stranger yanked him up by his collar, saving his life.

Robert recognized the famous actor right away, but Edwin didn't realize whom he had saved until he got a thank-you note from the president.

Saving the life of Lincoln's son was said to have been of some comfort to Edwin after the assassination.

Vincent & Theo van Gogh

When Your Brother
Is *Impossible*

Rude, arrogant, disagreeable, a total slob—that was Vincent van Gogh on a good day. His brother Theo could have told you about what he was like on a bad day: a pain in the neck, and everywhere else.

Vincent is one of the most famous painters who ever lived. As for Theo, he is famous as the saintly brother who worried about Vincent. In the history of unselfish brothers, Theo van Gogh probably takes the cake.

Theo, four years younger, was a fan from the get-go: "I adored him more than anything imaginable." Vincent taught Theo how to fish and ice-skate and play games like marbles. Later he poured energy into guiding his little brother's reading and education in art.

But even as a kid, Vincent was incredibly rebellious. As more and more people—including Mr. and Mrs. Van Gogh—didn't want to deal with the just plain impossible Vincent, Theo took on a parental role, feeling responsible for him and as though he had to be the "good son" to compensate.

In 1872, when Vincent was nineteen and Theo was fifteen, the Dutch brothers met over a pitcher of milk for a heart-to-heart chat. They talked excitedly about their futures and swore eternal friendship to each other. Siblings united.

A few days later Theo got a letter: "My dear Theo," it began. It was the first of what were going to be hundreds of famous letters in which Vincent poured his tortured heart out.

While Theo was making his mark as an art dealer, Vincent was a total bohemian, desperately poor, drifting from job to job.

He thought of being a minister like his father, and for a time he worked as a missionary in an impoverished mining region in Belgium, where he sketched people from the community. He was trying to follow in his father's footsteps, but going about it so eccentrically that his prim and proper father was appalled. Vincent wanted to live like those he preached to, sleeping on straw in a small hut at the back of the local baker's house. The baker's wife reported hearing Vincent sobbing at night, cold and hungry.

Vincent might have drifted into all-out oblivion if not for another heart-to-heart with Theo. In a fateful, honest discussion, Theo told him how much pain he was causing the family. Why couldn't he just settle down and take up a useful trade—librarian, baker, barber, *anything* respectable? Please?

Always thin-skinned, Vincent seemed to take the nudge as a stab in the back. He didn't write to Theo for nine months, the longest gap in their letters. Then Theo, out of pity, sent some money. Vincent responded with his longest letter ever, suddenly declaring that he was determined to be an artist. It was his final decision, his turning point.

He started filling sketchbook after sketchbook and devoted the rest of his life to art. Not necessarily respectable, but at least it was a focus.

Theo devoted the rest of *his* life to supporting his brother in his new goal. At one point he urged him to paint with oils— which was how Vincent would end up making his breakthroughs.

Vincent battled bitterly with everyone in their family except for Theo—especially their dad. One month after their dad's death, in 1885, Vincent painted a major work. Coincidence? In any case, *The Potato Eaters* is considered his first masterpiece.

This might have been the best year of Vincent's life, as close as he came to being content. He was making progress with his art—and maybe also in love. But that part didn't go well. The object of his affection, his landlady's daughter, rejected him outright, and Vincent grew further isolated and eccentric.

Romance was not his forte. Sometimes he was a bit of a stalker, as when he became obsessed with Kee, his recently widowed cousin. He proposed marriage but was refused with a pretty definite "No, nay, never." Undeterred, he still kept trying to see her. No go. Her parents disapproved—because Vincent was clearly unable to support himself. They wrote that his "persistence is disgusting." In desperation, he put his hand in the flame of a lamp, begging: "Let me see her for as long as I can keep my hand in the flame."

Not the best maneuver to win over worried parents—and Vincent continued his downward spiral in relationships.

He succeeded in burning all his bridges with people except for Theo, who observed, "It is a pity that he is his own enemy, for he makes life hard not only for others but for himself."

Vincent wasn't dense—he was aware of his own unlikability: "Don't imagine . . . that I believe it isn't my fault that many people find me a disagreeable character. I'm often and terribly cantankerously melancholic, irritable—yearning for sympathy as if with a kind of hunger and thirst." He ascribed his symptoms to "nervousness."

Bread, coffee, and tobacco were his daily diet, topped with absinthe, a potent green alcohol that made him hallucinate. By the time he was thirty-three, he looked fifty. Once, he wrote to Theo that he could remember eating only six hot meals since May of the previous year. Another time he lived for four days on twenty-three cups of coffee and a few crusts of bread. His teeth became loose and painful. After ten of them fell out, Theo made sure he got a dental plate so he could at least chew.

Anxiety about his brother never ceased.

Letters were really the only way to cope with Vincent. The brothers once tried living together in a Paris apartment—colossal mistake. Theo liked a quiet, well-ordered life. Vincent left open tubes of paint around next to his raggedy underwear, used Theo's socks to wipe off his canvases, and kept him up talking all night, following him from room to room.

After two years, Theo was ready to tear his hair out: "There was a time when I loved Vincent dearly and he was my best friend but that is no longer the case. . . . He never misses a chance of showing his contempt for me and telling me that I fill him with loathing. This makes sharing an apartment with him almost unbearable."

Worst roommate ever.

Vincent had *almost* managed to alienate the one person who believed in him. But Theo persisted in recognizing his brother's genius and never lost faith that his art would be "sublime."

Vincent took off for Arles, in southern France, and entered his most prolific period. He wrote Theo that if one day his paintings were good enough, "you will have been as much their creator as I, because the two of us are making them together."

Vincent did appreciate his worshipful brother: "How curious it is that you and I often seem to have the same thoughts." Their relationship meant everything to him.

Theo worked hard at his day job, selling art he didn't like nearly as much as his brother's. But his real job was worrying, making sure Vincent was okay financially and emotionally, buying his art supplies, giving him his old clothes, and sending fellow artist Paul Gauguin as a roommate (big mistake).

Over time, Vincent's behavior became more baffling and self-destructive. After a fight with Paul Gauguin, he injured himself.

It's the one thing many people know about Vincent: that one night he took a razor to his left ear—yes, according to the most recent research, the entire ear. He was found bleeding and unconscious the next day by the police and taken to the hospital.

The diagnosis was "generalized delirium"—in other words, doctors didn't know what was wrong.

Theo came immediately and laid his head on his brother's pillow in sorrow. As Vincent was recovering, he wrote to Theo, "Never lose courage, and remember how much I want you."

Vincent carried on with his art in the face of overwhelming rejection—and also taunting and bullying from townspeople who didn't understand him. In just over a decade, he produced more than 2,100 pieces, including around 860 oil paintings and more than 1,300 watercolors, drawings, sketches, and prints.

No one wanted them. In his whole life he sold only one painting.

Vincent realized (correctly) that he would never marry, but at age thirty-five he gave Theo permission to do so. Theo had fallen for a lovely woman named Jo. His brother tried to be cordial, but now there were three in the relationship—nothing was the same, especially after the couple had a baby, whom they named after him. Theo did his best, wanting Jo to see Vincent as "an advisor and brother to both of us, in every sense of the word." Vincent went along, and after this he addressed his letters to the two of them.

Theo was much more careful about saving their letters—surprise—and that's why we have some 660 letters revealing Vincent's insights and theories of art. Yes, he wrote profuse thank-yous for all the support, but he also wrote down complex thoughts about life, art, brotherhood. Often he wrote Theo every day or even twice a day. He would describe each painting he was working on—wheat fields, sunflowers, the starry sky. If he didn't tell Theo about it, it wasn't real or complete for him.

Mental illness was little understood then, and experts have debated fiercely about Vincent's illness and its effect on his work. Some thirty different diagnoses have been proposed, any of which could have been made worse by his horrible lifestyle—malnutrition, overwork, and too much alcohol, especially absinthe, the "green fairy."

In 1890, when Vincent was thirty-seven, Theo was facing a crisis in *his* career. He knew he was being treated unfairly at his job, and he was threatening to leave it. This would certainly have provoked a crisis for Vincent too—namely the end of his financial support.

Vincent was torn by guilt at his dependency: "I feared . . . that being a burden to you, you felt me to be rather a thing to be dreaded."

The conflict was too much. That same month he apparently shot himself in the stomach.

The following morning, Theo rushed to his brother's bedside

and found him awake and alert, smoking his pipe. But within hours Vincent began to fail. He died that evening, cradled in Theo's arms. "The sadness will last forever" were his last words.

Theo was crushed: "Oh, how empty it is everywhere. I miss him so: everything seems to remind me of him."

It was almost as though he couldn't go on without his brother to worry over. His own health declined rapidly. He died six months later, at age thirty-three, and was buried in the Dutch city of Utrecht.

It was Jo to the rescue. To honor Theo's wishes, she devoted the rest of her life to establishing Vincent's reputation. It was the publication of those amazing letters that was the determining factor in Vincent finally getting recognition as an artist. In 1914, the year she had their letters published, Jo had Theo's body moved from Utrecht and reburied with Vincent's in a suburb of Paris.

The Van Gogh brothers were together again—forever.

Serious Money

By the mid-twentieth century, Vincent was considered one of the greatest, most influential, and most recognizable painters in history.

His works are among the priciest paintings ever sold—any one of which could have kept him (and Theo) comfortable.

His *Self-Portrait with Bandaged Ear* sold for an estimated $90 million.

Many others have fetched similar prices.

A New Word: "Necronym"

Vincent was given the name of a brother who'd been born stillborn exactly a year before his own birth. It was haunting—he would have passed a tombstone with his own name on it every time he went to church.

But the practice of necronyms—reusing the name of a dead child for a younger sibling—was not unusual. Other famous bearers of necronyms are Ludwig van Beethoven and Salvador Dalí.

New Clues

In recent years scholars have proposed a new theory about Vincent's death. Was it really a suicide? Or was he a victim of manslaughter or foul play by two local bullies?

Most biographers still tend toward the suicide theory. He suffered from mental illness aggravated by his deep concern for Theo.

Wilbur & Orville Wright

"Just a Pair of Poor Nuts"

Wilbur and Orville Wright were not zany, not the most colorful characters to catch the world's attention. They were sixty shades of normal—wholesome homebodies who didn't drink, smoke, gamble, or date. And yet, what this occasionally quarrelsome couple did changed the world—forever and with flying colors.

It all started with a toy. When the brothers were age seven and eleven, their father brought home a gift that he tossed into the air. "Instead of falling to the floor, as we expected," the brothers recalled later, "it flew across the room till it struck the ceiling, where it fluttered awhile, and finally sank to the floor."

The model helicopter, powered by a rubber band, mesmerized the boys. Wilbur and Orville played with it until it broke and then built their own.

That became their pattern—tinkering, breaking toys, and putting them back together as a team. Their mom loved to build things with them—once constructing a sled—and they went to her, not their dad, when something needed repair.

Their dad, a bishop, kept the house teeming with encyclopedias and great books of every kind. The whole family, including two older brothers and Katharine, their younger sister, hung out at the public library in Dayton, Ohio.

Wilbur and Orville grew up as a unit—extraordinary role models for how to get along. Wilbur was much more dominant—he was the big brother, the leader (and their dad's clear favorite). He wrote better and was a better public speaker. But Orville was no slouch, and he and Wilbur were big on mutual respect, careful to share whatever brainstorms and opportunities came their way. When Wilbur was eighteen he was smashed in the face with a hockey stick. The blow knocked out all his upper front teeth and traumatized him. Instead of leaving Dayton for Yale University, which had been the plan, he stayed home for several years, a recluse. It was then that he really began reading intensely, getting obsessed with books about the flight of birds—and getting his brother equally obsessed.

Meanwhile, Orville, still tinkering, built his first printing press with scrap metal, a buggy spring, and oddly enough, a tombstone. (No one asked what made him think of that.) He urged Wilbur to get out of the house and join him, and in 1889 the brothers began to publish their own newspapers.

Three years later, in response to a national craze for bicycles, they switched gears and opened the Wright Cycle Company. Their successful bicycle repair and sales shop put them in just the right spot to continue their fixation with flight. With spare cash and lots of spare time, they financed their own flying experiments, relying on inexpensive materials (not tombstones), bicycle-inspired ideas about steering, and their own imaginations.

The brothers wrote to anyone who might tell them more, from the first experimenters to the Smithsonian Institution.

When Orville caught typhoid fever in 1896, Wilbur kept him entertained during his long recovery by reading him the newspaper. That's how they found out the story of the Flying Man, a German engineer who had been making brief flights in gliders of his own design. Unfortunately, he had just died—one of his gliders crashed. But his story lit a fire under the brothers, and they doubled down on their own experiments.

When the brothers worked together, they worked *together:* "Nearly everything that was done in our lives has been the result of conversations, suggestions, and discussions between us," Wilbur emphasized.

The most important woman in both brothers' lives was their younger sister. After their mother died, fourteen-year-old Katharine had taken charge of maintaining the household and providing moral support to her brothers still at home. (Two older brothers had married and moved away.) Said Orville, "When the world speaks of the Wrights, it must include our sister. Much of our effort has been inspired by her."

As well as the brothers got along, they also thrived on conflict. "I love to scrap with Orv," Wilbur said a bit gleefully—they spurred each other on. They often had blistering arguments—complete with shouting—about the right solution to the problem they were working on.

A niece reported overhearing them go back and forth in a way that sounds just like the arguments of little children:

"That's not so."

"'Tis too."

"'Tisn't either."

They would argue so long and so fiercely that something weird often happened. They could actually end up reversing their own positions, each having been convinced by the other.

But there was a method to their sibling madness, and they made progress.

Without having seen Kitty Hawk, part of North Carolina's Outer Banks, the brothers learned about its steady winds and lovely, wide beach.

So they left for Kitty Hawk. Katharine stayed behind to run the bicycle shop in their absence.

Local residents raised eyebrows as Wilbur and Orville stood

in the sand for hours at a time. What on Earth were they doing? Well, they were watching the giant seabirds soar along the beach. Then the brothers would flap along, using their own wrists and elbows to mimic the motion of the birds' wings. "We couldn't help thinking they were just a pair of poor nuts," said one local.

They finally arrived at a working model to test. When it came time to make the insanely risky test flights, they played fair and always took turns. They had promised their father, who rightfully feared losing both sons in an accident, that they would never fly together. They were never ones to engage in sibling daredevilry.

One day in 1903, it was Orville's turn, with Wilbur holding down his brother's coat so it wouldn't wrap itself around his head. Flying against the wind, staying aloft, Orville kept the plane in the air for twelve seconds.

It was man's first flight.

Over the next two years, they made another 150 flights, with constant breakthroughs. Weirdly, almost no one paid attention until 1906, when *Scientific American* acknowledged the brothers . . . by rudely challenging their honesty. If they had really flown, the magazine suggested, reporters surely would have let the world know by now. But those who were aware of their efforts either didn't believe what they heard or, if they investigated, didn't even believe what they were seeing.

The brothers persisted in the face of the disbelief, carrying on as a unit. They lived in the same house, worked together six days a week, ate their meals together, kept their money in a joint bank account, spoke exactly the same way—they even "thought together," said Wilbur. Both had a wonderful sense of humor.

Both were musical—Orville played mandolin, Wilbur the harmonica—and sometimes they started whistling or humming the same song *at the same time.*

Neither brother ever married or, apparently, had romantic attachments. They seemed wedded to their work. Wilbur told reporters that he didn't have time for both a wife and an airplane.

Katharine was there to keep them in line, and the bond between her and her two brothers was unbreakable. Intelligent, funny, with strong opinions, more sociable than her brothers, she became a high school teacher. She didn't fly until six years after they did but followed their work closely. She did have a temper, which was sometimes aimed at her brothers. But she was there when they needed her, always.

The brothers were finally on the road to establishing their credibility when they sold one of their airplanes to the United States Army in 1908. Orville set about running tests on the army plane. A few minutes into a flight he was demonstrating at Fort Myer, in Virginia, the propeller disintegrated. The plane smashed into the ground at full speed. His passenger died. Orville was hospitalized for six weeks with a broken leg, four broken ribs, and a back injury that plagued him for the rest of his life.

Katharine immediately took an indefinite leave of absence from her teaching job, got on the train, stayed by his side, and did everything she could to comfort and encourage him. He said later that he couldn't have recovered without her.

A month earlier, Wilbur had demonstrated the first public flight in France—and the brothers were becoming internationally famous. On later trips to France, they were treated as heroes, respected more than they were in America.

When Katharine accompanied her brothers to Europe, French newspapers were fascinated by her, so much more outgoing and charming than her siblings. Rumors began to exaggerate her importance in the invention of the plane, despite consistent denials by her and the brothers.

In France, when they weren't demonstrating their plane to the public, they spent all their free time mastering a popular French toy called the *diabolo*. *"Les frères mystérieux,"* whispered the French—the mysterious brothers. Soon the most popular toy in France was a replica of their plane.

Back in Dayton, the Wright Company established a factory for manufacturing planes. All three siblings became huge celebrities. Compared to the sizzle of inventing, being famous was a chore for the brothers. Wilbur resented the time spent "answering the ten thousand fool questions people ask me about the machine." Lawsuits with other inventors challenging their claims took up too much of their energy.

Wilbur had his regrets: "When we think what we might have accomplished if we had been able to devote this time to experiments, we feel very sad, but it is always easier to deal with things than with men, and no one can direct his life entirely as he would choose."

In 1910, Orville took their eighty-two-year-old father on his first and only flight. As the plane gained elevation, his excited father cried out, "Higher, Orville, higher!" Luckily, this was not a flight that crashed.

The brothers' personalities never changed, and nothing turned their heads. They were the most famous human beings on Earth at the time, but they didn't start dressing fancy or hobnobbing with the rich and glamorous. All they really wanted to do was get back to work. Any money they earned, they spent on more experiments.

Worn out from fighting lawsuits, Wilbur died of typhoid in 1912, at age forty-five. His adoring father wrote in his diary: "A short life, full of consequences. An unfailing intellect, imperturbable temper, great self-reliance and as great modesty, seeing the right clearly, pursuing it steadfastly, he lived and died."

Orville carried on their work, ever polite and reserved, saying little about the loss of his beloved brother. Katharine took on some of Wilbur's business responsibilities, becoming an officer of the Wright Company.

She devoted herself to Orville—until one day she didn't. Finally carving out a life for herself, she married at age fifty-two. Orville couldn't handle the change. He felt so betrayed that he stopped speaking to her. Two years later, Katharine contracted pneumonia. Orville still refused to reach out. . . . Another brother finally persuaded him to visit her, and Orville was at her bedside when she died, at fifty-four years old.

Orville did stay close to his enormous Saint Bernard, Scipio, and made toys for nieces and nephews, tinkering with other inventions and fighting with lawyers. He died thirty-five years after his brother, at seventy-six, in 1948, following his second heart attack.

Today we think of them as one unit: the Wright brothers. The brothers had done *everything* together except die at the same time.

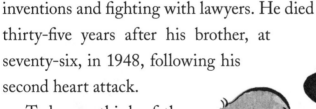

Wilbur, Not Always Right

The Wrights grew up without indoor plumbing, electricity, or a telephone—it was an era desperate for inventions. While they worked on their plane, elevators, sewing machines, and cars also came along.

Wilbur wasn't always optimistic about progress—he didn't see any future in the automobile, and in 1901 he said he didn't think man would fly for another fifty years.

Who Was Better?

The brothers always presented a unified image to the public, equally sharing the credit for their invention.

But most historians, digging further, agree that Wilbur was the leader, from the beginning to the end. He was the visionary, while Orville had the passion to help him carry out the vision.

The brothers saw their invention as being of great possible benefit to humanity, thinking in grand terms.

"We dared to hope we had invented something that would bring lasting peace to the earth," Orville said. "But we were wrong."

Not long after Wilbur's death, planes began playing their destructive role in World War I.

By World War II, they were weapons causing deaths on an unforeseen scale.

Walt & Roy Disney

Making Your Kid Brother's Dreams Come True

Who doesn't love Walt Disney and his empire of warm, fuzzy family entertainment? But without his brother Roy, there would have been no Walt.

No Walt Disney!

Their childhood was not warm and fuzzy. Their dad was beyond strict with his four sons and basically saw them as moneymakers.

Roy was older than Walt by eight years, and from the beginning he sensed that Walt didn't have the common sense most kids did. It was his job to be Walt's protector. He pushed baby Walt around, and later their little sister Ruth. Roy took Walt to watch the trains passing by each day, and on hot days to the nearby creek for skinny-dipping. He bought Walt toys and candy out of his own money, took him to movies, and played horseshoes with him.

About one thing they were in agreement. Said Roy: "He was a pet around the house." Walt smirked: "I was sort of the pet in the family."

Walt discovered his love for drawing when a neighbor in Marceline, Missouri, paid him a nickel to draw pictures of his horse Rupert.

No money in drawing, his father insisted (ha!). Instead, he put nine-year-old Walt to work with Roy on his delivery route for the *Kansas City Star*. The Disney brothers woke up at 4:30 a.m. and delivered hundreds of newspapers until the school bell rang, then went back to work after school until dinner. They never got to keep the money they earned—Dad said they owed it to the family.

Walt found the paper route exhausting and often fell asleep

in class, harming his grades. He kept it up for more than six years but for forty years afterward still had nightmares about missing customers on his route.

Roy was a comfort, like a substitute father: "We were great pals, and anything that happened I'd tell him. I never kept anything from Roy." They did have fights, but over small things, like Walt borrowing Roy's ties and spilling chili and beans on them. At night they slept in the same bed and told each other stories.

The Disney brothers tell different stories about their dad's treatment. Beatings and whippings were his idea of discipline. Most telling of all: Walt's older brothers Herbert and Ray, fed up with the constant work and lack of spending money, went out a bedroom window and disappeared in 1906.

About Walt, Roy claimed, "Us older kids said that he got off easy with Dad because by the time Dad got around to him he'd worn himself out chasing us, so Walt had an easy time." Walt might have disagreed. He couldn't help arguing with his dad and talking back. Sometimes, he would have to push a chair in between them for temporary protection.

One day, as fourteen-year-old Walt was headed down to the basement for a beating, Roy urged him to physically stand up to their dad. He did, and his dad never threatened him again.

Plotting his escape, Walt attended art classes wherever and whenever he could, looking for chances to use his growing skill as an animation artist.

In 1917, Roy joined the navy to fight in World War I. Walt was anxious to follow him, but he was only sixteen, too young for the military. So Walt lied about his age and spent a year driving a Red Cross ambulance in France.

Upon discharge, Roy was hospitalized with tuberculosis in Los Angeles. Walt, by then eighteen, traveled to see him about an exciting offer he'd received, asking for his brother's help. Roy left the hospital the next day, against medical advice, starting his career as a banker and BFF to Walt.

Walt had succeeded in opening his own animation business, creating cartoons called Laugh-O-Grams. He studied *Aesop's Fables* as a model for his modernized fairy tales and, with Roy's help, wanted to start making movies.

In 1923 the brothers teamed up and founded Disney Brothers Studio in Hollywood—entering a partnership that would last forty-three years.

Roy was the respectable one, while Walt was a starving artist, subsisting on new ideas. He had to go to Roy to get money for paper to draw on. He slept on some cushions when he had to and

once went three days without a meal. At the cheapest cafeteria, the brothers worked out a system: one would choose the meat, the other the vegetable, and then they'd share, considering it a square meal between them.

The two tried living together, but the experiment fizzled. Roy did the cooking, and Walt turned up his nose. He moved out after an argument about the meals.

But Walt didn't have to cook for himself too long. Both brothers got married almost immediately. They ordered and built kit houses, side by side on Lyric Avenue in Los Angeles. Walt and his wife had a daughter and adopted another; Roy and his wife had a son.

Walt was always wanting to try things that had never been done before, always in financial hot water, on the verge of going under. One bad habit, for example, was not reading contracts. Time and time again, Roy found ways to bail him out: "Junior's got his hand in the cookie jar again," he said with good humor.

It was always clear that Walt was the company's spark, and Roy was happy for Walt to earn nearly twice as much as he did because of that fact. At first they worked in a studio on Hyperion Avenue in Los Angeles, the two of them plus seven employees.

Their big break came with short films starring Mickey Mouse, a mischievous cartoon character based on a mouse Walt had once adopted as a pet. Walt did the voice of Mickey himself at first and felt in some ways that he *was* Mickey.

Mickey's success gave Walt enough credibility and cash to try something nerve-racking: making the first feature-length cartoon movie. Walt called a meeting to share his version of *Snow White and the Seven Dwarfs* with his staff, now numbering 250 employees, and enacted all the parts himself. Roy held on for the ride: the animation technique required more than 200,000 separate drawings and cost more than $34 million in today's dollars.

The bet paid off. *Snow White* earned $117 million in today's dollars, as well as a permanent spot in movie history. It began an era known as the Golden Age of Animation for the studio. Walt and Roy used *Snow White* profits to build a splendid new complex of offices and production facilities in Burbank, California.

Full speed ahead on one outrageously creative project after another. Walt was always in the office when Roy arrived and there when he left: "He was a bear for work."

Said Roy, "I just try to keep up with him—and make it pay." His job was to be practical while trying not to squelch Walt's enthusiasm—a tricky brotherly balancing act: "Nothing was done that would ever hurt the business or would hurt Walt. I protected that with a fervor." It helped that Roy was never jealous, always proud. Besides being a master storyteller, his brother was a pioneer, elevating animation into an art form with characters the audience could connect with on an emotional level.

Roy once tried to contribute creatively, questioning Walt's choice of music for his wildly experimental film *Fantasia*. After a long pause, Walt gave him a look. "Roy," he said, "*we'll* make the pictures, *you* get the money." That was the end of that conversation.

While Walt was constantly reinventing, they rarely disagreed, except when Roy thought he was simply thinking too big. "We had quite a screamer," Walt said about one argument. After any conflict they felt bad and settled their differences. Both had healthy senses of humor. Trying to calm Walt down, Roy would say, "Look, you're letting this place drive you nuts—that's one place I'm not going with you."

Roy was skeptical of Walt's ambitious plans for Disneyland, for example. So Walt took out loans and formed his own separate company to do outside projects. This led to months of strife, their worst falling-out, with several tense moments of not being on speaking terms. Walt finally sold the other company—"I love you," he wrote in his letter, making peace—and Roy went on to put together the financing deals for the spectacularly successful theme park in Anaheim, California.

One night, speaking at a dinner, Walt admitted, "If it hadn't been for my big brother, I swear I've been in jail several times for checks bouncing. I never knew what was in the bank. He kept me on the straight and narrow."

So what did Roy get out of it? Extremely camera shy, he dreaded the publicity and fame that came with being Walt's brother. But Roy was able to feed off Walt's creativity—he could have been just a boring banker otherwise. Mainly, it was the satisfaction of helping his kid brother: "My job all along was to help Walt do the things he wanted to do. He did the dreaming. I did the building."

Not to mention that he also made a good living. The brothers lived well; they were able to look past their dad's anger management issues and stay close to their parents, building them a dream house in California. Their older brothers had resurfaced, and Walt and Roy were generous with all their siblings.

By the early 1960s, the Disney empire had established itself as the world's leading producer of family entertainment. Cutting-edge at first, it became mainstream—beloved by all.

Nearing seventy, Roy was eager to retire, but then Walt had his biggest brainstorm ever—the extravagant Walt Disney World, near Orlando, Florida. At a luncheon, Walt was asked what the effect would be on the Florida project if he got hit by a truck after lunch. Walt replied, "Absolutely nothing. My brother Roy runs this company. I just piddle around."

But soon after, Walt found out he had lung cancer. As he got sicker, Roy came to the hospital every day, rubbing his feet when he complained of being cold, sitting with him until the end. Walt, Roy reported, was working up until the day he died.

He was staring at the pattern of tiles on the hospital ceiling, with every four tiles representing a square mile, and envisioning the map for Disney World, plotting where attractions would go.

On the day Walt died, at sixty-five, in 1966, Roy sobbed uncontrollably. His daughter reported him saying, "Well, kid, this is the end, I guess."

Roy was never the same. "I am so sad," he said after losing his brother and business partner—a true case of sibling devotion.

He longed to travel and spend time with his grandchildren. Instead, in true-blue big-brother fashion, he oversaw the completion of Disney World. He spent five years in the heat and humidity of Florida, wrestling to tame swampland and scrub brush, tackling construction delays and risky finances to make Walt's last dream a reality.

The park opened in 1971. That same year, Roy died at age seventy-eight of a stroke.

The Disney brothers are gone, but what they created together lives on—particularly in the hearts of today's children who treasure the Disney magic.

Big Brothers of America

When Walt gave a speech in honor of Big Brothers, a program giving one-on-one guidance for boys in need, he talked about his own mentor: "My father . . . never understood me. He thought I was the black sheep. This nonsense of drawing pictures! . . .

"But my big brother would say, 'Kid, go ahead!' . . . I was fortunate. I had a big brother. And he's still with me. And I still love him. I argue with him. Sometimes I think he's the stubbornest so-and-so I ever met in my life. But I don't know what the hell I'd do without him."

From Small Beginnings

In 1933 Roy wrote home: "Just think, there are about 130 or 135 people around here, living on Mickey Mouse. He's a pretty good mouse, don't you think, to keep up so many families?"

As of 2013, the company had annual revenues of over $45 billion and employed approximately 175,000 people. The Walt Disney Company owns five vacation resorts, eleven theme parks, and much, much more. It is by far the world's largest operator of theme parks, and its motion picture studio is still one of the six major film studios in Hollywood.

Debunking the Most Famous Disney Myth

According to an urban legend, Walt was cryopreserved. (Cryopreservation is a method of freezing the body in the belief that it can be brought back to life at a later date.)

Could his frozen corpse be stored beneath the Pirates of the Caribbean ride at Disneyland?

No.

WALTER ELIAS DISNEY
LILIAN BOUNDS DISNEY
ROBERT B. BROWN
SHARON DISNEY BROWN

Walt was cremated and his ashes buried at the Forest Lawn Memorial Park—joined by Roy's after his death.

The Romanovs

The Doomed Siblings

Before the Russian Revolution of 1917, life for the five royal Romanov children was a happily-ever-after fairy tale, a non-stop party. You might well ask: Were the Romanovs some of the most spoiled children on Earth?

All the adults around them pampered them, but they didn't even have to be around adults. The children had their very own island on the lush grounds of their favorite palace, with their own little house and child-sized furniture. In the summer they took bike rides, rowed boats, rode ponies, played with dozens of pets, including eleven English collies. Winters were for sledding, building snowmen and castles, skiing.

Each one had a Kodak Brownie camera, cutting-edge technology at that time, and they delighted in taking dozens of pictures a day of themselves frolicking—perhaps the first selfies. After dinner they pasted their photos into deluxe albums of green Moroccan leather while their dad read aloud to them. Their five hundred servants met their every need—they even included a librarian, who supplied Dad with twenty of the best books from around the world each month.

The children lived blissfully and totally secluded from the real world. "It is very pleasant to spend [time] in a small family circle," said their doting dad.

"Dad" was the Russian tsar Nicholas II, who ruled over 130 million people and one-sixth of the planet. He was the richest monarch in the world—living like, well, a king—on money he took from his poor subjects. He owned thirty palaces, millions of acres of land, gold and silver mines, yachts, private trains, and jewels beyond measure. He was also the head of the Russian Orthodox Church, so his power was unlimited on Earth *and* in heaven.

Most of his subjects

were starving, but anyone who spoke against him was exiled to faraway frozen Siberia.

The four oldest Romanov siblings were girls. With Russian law forbidding women to rule, each was a slight disappointment, and all awaited a boy.

The girls didn't let their lack of power ruin their fairy tale. They danced through their days in beautiful white dresses with colored sashes, their thick, glossy hair tied back with satin bows. Their perfumes were specially made for them in Paris—rose, jasmine, lilac, and violet. They played with lavish dolls sent by their great-great-grandma, Queen Victoria of England.

The girls were homeschooled by their mom, Tsarina Alexandra, and private tutors. But since they weren't going to be in charge, they were allowed to do just enough to get by, learning a little basic math, a little science, and a lot of religion. They were supposed to study the four languages that were in use around court, but only Olga really mastered them.

The four were so sheltered that in some ways they never really grew up. Even as they moved into their teens, they talked and behaved like little girls.

Once, when two of them had the chance to go shopping in a store, they realized that they didn't know how to buy anything—they had never used money.

The oldest, Olga, was only six years older than the youngest, Anastasia.

Olga was gifted at the piano and probably the most well read, keeping up with the newspapers. She even liked to put her stamp of approval on novels her mom wanted to read. Kindhearted, she once threw her fancy doll out of the sleigh to a poor crying girl she saw by the side of the road. She was keenly aware of being the oldest, constantly pressured to be an example for the others.

On her sixteenth birthday, her parents gave Olga diamond jewelry and threw her a full dress ball. While everyone gossiped about her future marriage prospects with princes, Olga was more inclined to flirt with army officers. Her goal was modest, and the opposite of royal: "To get married, live always in the countryside winter and summer, always mix with good people, and no officialdom whatsoever."

At twenty, Olga began to use part of her enormous inheritance for charitable causes. As war and revolution brewed, she paid more attention to the outside world and was more aware than most in her family of how much Russians were turning against her parents. She often appeared sad and worried.

You'd think Olga would have been her mom's favorite, but that was Tatiana. She was eighteen months younger, a take-charge kind of person, especially skilled at scanning her mother's moods and responding appropriately. It was Tatiana whom the girls sent as their representative when they wanted their parents to grant a favor.

As the middle child, Maria seemed to be a scapegoat. Perhaps out of some form of sibling rivalry, she got picked on so much by her sisters, even the youngest one, that she had to be specially watched. No wonder she sometimes felt insecure and left out. The sisters objected to including Maria in their games and referred to her as "stepsister" (a harsh thing to call your biological sister). They nicknamed her "fat little bow-wow." She was surprisingly strong and sometimes amused herself by demonstrating how she could lift her tutors off the ground.

Perhaps Maria inspired resentment because she never got into trouble. Once, she stole some biscuits from her mother's tea table. As a punishment, Alexandra wanted to banish her to bed, but Nicholas excused her: "I was always afraid of the wings growing. I am glad to see she is only a human child."

Anastasia, the youngest sister, was Maria's opposite. Outgoing and afraid of nothing, she was often deliberately disobedient, eating apples she was told not to, or climbing trees and refusing to come down. Her cousins complained that when she didn't get her way, Anastasia was "nasty to the point of being evil." She loathed school and was rumored to have tried to strangle her teacher. Once, playing a practical "joke" during a snowball fight, Anastasia rolled a rock into a snowball and threw it at Tatiana, knocking her to the ground. A talented mimic, she would hide underneath the bear rug in the sleigh and bark like a dog or cluck like a hen.

Finally, finally, as the girls began moving into their teens, a son was born in 1904—at last, an heir. But to everyone's horror, Alexei had inherited hemophilia, an incurable disease that prevents blood from clotting normally. Before modern medical treatments, life expectancy for hemophiliacs was only about thirteen years.

It was crucial that Alexei not injure himself—even a trivial injury such as a bruise, a nosebleed, or a cut could be painful and life threatening. Two navy sailors monitored him at all times and, as injuries were still unavoidable, carried him around when he was unable to walk during his long recoveries.

It was also crucial that his illness was kept a state secret so that the powers of the Romanov dynasty wouldn't come under question. Keeping Alexei's secret had the effect of isolating the family even further.

The acute pain he suffered tortured his parents. He couldn't take aspirin or morphine, so his only relief was to pass out.

Tsarina Alexandra, a deeply religious woman, came to rely on a mysterious faith healer named Rasputin. No one really knows how, but Rasputin did seem to help Alexei where conventional doctors had failed. He became the only person around them they could trust. The siblings were taught to call Rasputin "Our Friend" and confide in him. The not-very-trustworthy Rasputin was able to gain influence over the Romanovs—for his own benefit.

All the illnesses and recoveries interfered with Alexei's education—he hated lessons and was even less well educated than his sisters.

He was aware that he might not live to adulthood. When he was ten, Olga found him looking at the clouds: "I like to think and wonder," he said. Olga asked him what he liked to think about. "Oh, so many things," the boy said. "I enjoy the sun and the beauty of summer as long as I can."

Alexei still found ways to be as mischievous as anyone else, or maybe more so. He threw pellets of bread at his dad's guards and played pranks on guests. At one formal dinner party, he removed the shoe of a woman from under the table and showed it to his father. Nicholas ordered him to return his "trophy," which Alexei did, but not before placing a large, juicy strawberry into the toe of the shoe. Olga was held responsible for Alexei's behavior at the table and restrained him from licking his plate, slouching, teasing.

Even when Alexei was a toddler, his father began to prepare him for his future role as tsar by inviting him to sit in on long meetings with government ministers.

He lorded his status over the others. At age six, he told his sisters, "Now, girls, run away. I am busy. Someone has just called to see me on business." At eleven he complained of being "the only man amongst all these women."

Kind of obnoxious.

The girls were affectionate with him but remained a tight unit, despite minor squabbles and rivalries, sharing a collective identity that didn't include their brother. Sometimes they signed letters using the nickname OTMA, which came from the first letters of their first names.

The overwhelming concern for Alexei diverted the attention of the Romanovs from the Russian Revolution and civil war, erupting as people became fed up with having so little while the royal family had so much.

All were caught by surprise and sorrow in March 1917. The entire family, even the children, was arrested and imprisoned at their palace. Electricity, phone service, and the water supply were cut off, and most of their staff deserted them. If they stepped outside, angry crowds gathered to attack. Rasputin had been murdered a few months earlier by those who hated his sway over the royal family, and no one was coming to their rescue.

Packing up luxurious possessions, including at least $14 million in jewels, they were moved to private residences for their own safety. Finally they were moved to the House of Special Purpose, in the far-off, dreaded Siberia.

Under house arrest, the siblings grew closer than ever. For a time, their biggest enemy was boredom, which they tried to head off by reading, sewing, playing cards, trying to keep warm, and praying for rescue as this civil war played out. The children did

all they could to cheer up their parents, especially Tatiana and Anastasia, who put on plays to make them laugh.

Maria passed the time by attempting to befriend guards. She showed them pictures from her photo albums and talked with them about their families and her hopes for a new life in England when she was released.

One guard smuggled in a birthday cake to celebrate Maria's nineteenth birthday, on June 26, 1918. He was removed from his position, and the conditions of their imprisonment became even more strict.

The girls took turns keeping their mother company. Alexei, confined to bed in severe pain after his latest injury, played toy soldiers with a young kitchen assistant. Olga seemed deeply depressed and lost a great deal of weight. A guard recalled that the few times she walked outside, she stood there "gazing sadly into the distance."

Life got smaller and smaller. On July 4, a harsh new leader arrived, barking orders to the family. Anastasia stuck her tongue out at him when he turned his back and left the room.

On July 13, Alexei felt well enough to take his first bath in nine weeks.

On July 15, Olga and her sisters joked with one another and moved the beds in their room so that visiting cleaning women could scrub the floor.

On the night of July 16, the family, plus their doctor, cook, and two servants, was awakened. They were told to go down to the basement, that there was unrest in the town and they would have to be moved again. Anastasia refused to leave her spaniel behind.

The family was taken inside a room and informed that they were to be photographed to prove to the public that they were still alive. The family members were arranged appropriately and left alone for several minutes. Then gunmen walked in and started shooting.

The Russian Revolution was a world cataclysm, changing Russia into the Soviet Union, from a monarchy into a Communist state. In the process, it killed 13 million people—including our royal siblings: Olga, age twenty-two; Tatiana, twenty-one; Maria, nineteen; Anastasia, seventeen; and Alexei, thirteen.

A Source of Unending Rumors

The bodies of the Romanovs were handled carelessly, hidden, and moved several times before being buried in an unmarked pit. In 1991, all but two of the bodies were dug up. Multiple laboratories in different countries confirmed their identity through DNA testing. But where were the other two?

Not until 2007 were the bodies of Alexei and Maria discovered nearby. They had probably been removed to lighten the load when the truck carrying the bodies got stuck in the mud.

The Impostors

Many people, horrified at the thought of executing innocent children, wanted to believe that some of the Romanov siblings had escaped. Meanwhile, many impostors came forward claiming to have survived the mass murder.

The most famous was Anna Anderson, who insisted she was Anastasia. Though she was identified as a Polish factory worker with a history of mental illness, she had many supporters, including members of the royal family. Eventually, tests proved that her DNA didn't match that of the Romanov remains or of living relatives.

The five Romanovs found together were given a proper burial in 1998.

But as of 2016, the Russian Orthodox Church still refused to hold a funeral for Alexei and Maria, denying the authenticity of their remains for mysterious political reasons.

The eighty remaining descendants want the burial.

Meanwhile, the siblings' bone fragments rest inside two small white boxes in a Moscow vault.

The Kennedys

"We Don't Want Losers Around Here"

One day young Joe and Jack Kennedy had a bicycle race. As they were headed straight for each other, playing chicken, each refused to swerve out of the way. Crash! Ouch! Jack would need twenty-eight stitches, while Joe was just fine.

Believe it or not, the bike race had been their father's idea. "We want winners," Joseph Kennedy often declared. "We don't want losers around here." Even if they crashed into each other, apparently.

Glamorous, rich, and popular, the nine Kennedy siblings were

like no other American family, just what their dad, a billionaire businessman, demanded of them. The oldest, Joe Jr., was seventeen years older than the youngest, Edward (Teddy). In between were John (Jack), Rosemary, Kathleen (so lively that she was called Kick), Eunice, Patricia (Pat), Robert (Bobby), and Jean.

Their mom, Rose, seconded the no-losers motion. Winning at sports was as important as getting top grades: "They learned to be winners, not losers, in sports." If they lost a game, the siblings didn't get sympathy but instead intense analysis of what they'd done wrong.

Big things were expected of the four boys—doing great deeds, helping their country.

Joe was the shining star. Both parents made it obvious Joe was their favorite. When a third-grade teacher once called Rose to say Jack actually had a higher IQ, she insisted that the teacher had to be wrong. Everyone assumed Joe would go straight to the top, even become president—though the idea of an Irish Catholic in the White House was unthinkable at that time.

Great things were expected of the girls too, but more as wives and mothers—and public supporters of their brothers.

Joe took his role all too seriously: "You know I'm the oldest of my family, and I've got to be the example for a lot of brothers and sisters." They all saw him as a parental figure. As Jack wrote later, "Joe did many things well . . . but I have always felt that Joe achieved his greatest success as the oldest brother. . . . I think that

if the Kennedy children amount to anything now or ever . . . it will be due more to Joe's behavior and his constant example than to any other factor."

Among many other things, Joe taught them all how to sail the ocean on Cape Cod, at the family compound at Hyannisport, Massachusetts. All the siblings were expected to show a wide range of social and academic skills. Even playing was a skill—charades, Monopoly, skiing, horse riding, pillow fights, swimming, tennis, and, above all, touch football, for both girls and boys. How much guts could you show on the football field?

Visitors found it exhausting to keep up with them.

Rose ran a tight ship, organizing the family like a corporation, with an elaborate system of file cards noting statistics, birthdays, illnesses (which in Jack's case ran to numerous cards). If anyone misbehaved—even crying was frowned upon—one icy glare from their father (called "Daddy's look") was usually enough to squelch the behavior. He was so often away on business that when he was home, it was a big treat. Reading the newspaper comics aloud in bed, he would be covered in little snuggling Kennedys.

Every night at dinner, the teaching of skills continued. Rose lectured on the great men in history who they were to emulate. Each kid was expected to be able to debate current events. That meant they had to keep up with the news and be prepared to talk about that day's Supreme Court decision, events in Russia and the Middle East, discrimination against the Italians and the Irish. Whew—meals weren't just a matter of eating food but of surviving the pressure.

Magazines wrote articles about the "amazing Kennedys." All the one-upmanship and competition could have created friction. But the siblings were insanely proud of each other, inspiring one another, and they mostly acted without jealousy. One friend put it this way: "They fight each other, yet they feed on each other. They stimulate each other. Their minds strike sparks."

The main rivalry was between the two oldest, only twenty-two months apart. Around their neighborhood, Joe was Jack's protector. But at home—not so much. Jack read more books, but

Joe got better grades; plus, Joe was bigger, healthier, and better at football. He may have been a bit of a bully, sometimes deliberately throwing a ball at Jack hard enough to knock him down.

Still, Jack never stopped needling him. He might steal Joe's piece of chocolate pie when he wasn't looking. A fistfight would start, and Jack would lose—always. Yet he lived to tease, stubbornly believing that one of these days he'd win.

While Joe was being groomed for the presidency, Jack had less of a burden and more independence. But he dutifully followed Joe into college, law school, then military service during World War II (though, with his poor health, he had to fight to get accepted). He took on a parental role too, gathering his younger siblings around the fireplace and telling them about great leaders he'd read about.

Bobby needed the encouragement, for he struggled to keep up with his stellar siblings. "As the seventh of nine children in a competitive family," he said, "I had to keep getting better in every way just to survive." As a toddler he repeatedly hurled himself

into the ocean, trying in vain to teach himself to swim. Was it possible he thought sinking was preferable to facing his family if he couldn't swim? His siblings would rescue him—laughing—until he finally mastered the skill.

On after-school walks, Jack would tell Bobby about the daring deeds of Lawrence of Arabia or King Arthur, how one person really can change history. Bobby went from feeling he was inferior to being a fighter. Just as Jack fought his way into the navy, Bobby fought his way onto the Harvard football team, despite his small size and occasional serious injuries.

Bobby was the only one of the four brothers who met his father's offer of a thousand dollars if he didn't drink or smoke until age twenty-one.

When Teddy, the youngest Kennedy, was born, Jack asked to be the baby's godfather. He wanted to name the baby George Washington, but his parents overruled him.

In true Kennedy fashion, his brothers taught Teddy their best skills. All the brothers pressured each other, and he got the most pressure. How to make his mark in such a competitive family? Like many youngest siblings, Teddy grew up as the family clown, striving to cheer people up.

Once, when Teddy was being bullied at school, he asked Bobby for help. Bobby walked away, saying, "You've got to learn to fight your own battles." He wasn't trying to be mean—that *was* his way of helping.

One sibling, alas, didn't fit in. When she was about nine, their sister Rosemary's mental development seemed to stop. Together the others took care of her. Bobby played dodgeball with her; Jack made sure she danced at parties. Her sisters helped her dress and put on makeup and in public watched her for embarrassing or strange behavior.

As she entered her twenties, Rosemary was more and more frustrated at not being able to keep up with her glamorous siblings. She grew irrational and even violent, hitting people, having some kind of seizure. Doctors were confused by her intellectual disability, and her father agreed to an experimental brain surgery that backfired. She became physically disabled as well.

That was one great sorrow for the family. Another came when the family hero, Joe, died at age twenty-nine.

A year earlier, Jack was so intent on proving himself in the navy that he became a genuine war hero. After his boat, PT-109, was cut in half by a Japanese destroyer, he took courageous action to rescue his surviving crew, earning several medals for his bravery.

By then, Joe had completed so many navy combat missions as a fighter pilot that he was eligible to go home. Instead, still competitive with his little brother, he volunteered for one more bombing mission—and to everyone's horror he was shot down.

The loss stunned the whole family. The Kennedys in some ways never really recovered from losing their shining star.

Jack may have felt it most keenly—he had been so used to defining himself in opposition to Joe. Now, as he put it, "I'm shadowboxing in a match the shadow is always going to win."

Ready or not, according to Kennedy tradition, Jack had to take on his brother's role. Two years after Joe's death, Jack started to run for public office. The whole family pitched in and helped in every possible way.

Teddy, still in college, sometimes spoke for him when Jack's voice failed. If he was stuck in a traffic jam, he would jump out of the car and offer his brother's bumper stickers to the other drivers.

Bobby managed Jack's campaigns with eighteen-hour days. They became close friends, not competitors. Bobby could finish his brother's sentences and follow his gestures, then do what he wanted done.

Kick volunteered for the Red Cross, wrote her own newspaper column, and had a dazzling romantic life, with suitors her parents disapproved of. She seemed destined to accomplish much, but she died just three years after Joe, at age twenty-eight, in a plane

crash. The siblings mourned the loss of their buoyant, sparkling sister.

Great sorrows, great triumphs.

In 1960 Jack was elected, against all odds, to the presidency. He was the youngest man and the first Roman Catholic to be elected.

Bobby served as his attorney general and continued to influence him. He was the one who thought guaranteeing civil rights for African Americans was the most urgent problem in America and prodded Jack to take action.

When Jack was assassinated, one thousand days into his presidency, the siblings were devastated, and so was the country. It was a long time before Bobby could speak his name without crying.

In his saddest moments, he put on a navy sea jacket Jack had worn and talked to him aloud.

He took on the role of his older brother, running for office. But, while campaigning for president, he too was assassinated. His last words after being shot were "I'm hurt. No, no, no. Jack. Jack."

Teddy was now suddenly an elder in the family and the role model and protector for his dead brothers' many children. He didn't always handle his burden perfectly, but he was always there for his family and his country. Teddy became a senator at age thirty. His very first speech was on civil rights, continuing what Jack had started. The only Kennedy brother to live long enough to have gray hair, he forged ahead. He was known as the Lion

of the Senate—for forty-six years, Teddy worked on laws that helped just about everyone in America, especially the poorest people.

The surviving sisters, meanwhile, put in long hours behind the scenes on their brothers' campaigns, especially getting women out to vote. As opportunities for women expanded, the sisters moved onto the public stage too.

Eunice worked in various branches of government, married the American ambassador to France, and became a champion for children's health and disability issues. She helped found the Special Olympics, a global program to emphasize athletics in the lives of disabled children.

Pat's goal was to produce films, but Hollywood wasn't accepting of women behind the camera then; she worked as an assistant on movies, wrote newspaper articles, married a famous actor, Peter Lawford, and founded the National Committee for the Literary Arts.

As for Jean, the shyest, she became the American ambassador to Ireland and has outlived all her brothers and sisters.

With thirty children among the siblings—and more than one hundred grandchildren—the Kennedy winner-take-all spirit will surely live on.

Big Brother and Little Brother

In the famous novel *1984* by George Orwell, Big Brother is the hated leader of a state where everyone is under surveillance at all times.

Signs all over say "Big Brother is watching you."

As Jack's campaign manager and later as attorney general, Bobby fought so ferociously on behalf of his brother that some staff members felt bullied.

"Little Brother is watching you," they would complain.

Money—No Worries!

As much as their dad encouraged them to compete, the siblings didn't have to fight about money. When each of them turned twenty-one, Joe presented them with a fund worth over $1 million (approximately $16 million in today's dollars).

It was a way of investing in his own children and encouraging them to serve their country without having to obsess about money. Jack, our wealthiest president up until that time, always donated his government salaries to charity, as did Bobby and Ted.

Fighting Brothers

One study shows that brothers under the age of seven fight an average of every seventeen minutes.

This seems to have provided the perfect training ground for the seven pairs of American brothers who have won Olympic medals in boxing or wrestling.

Firstborns get to have their parents' undivided attention for a while.

This makes them somewhat parental themselves, and high achievers.

Firstborns are more likely to be presidents, Nobel Prize winners, explorers.

Of the first twenty-three American astronauts to explore space, twenty-one were the firstborn in their families.

Most Influential Sibling?

Dealing with Rosemary's special needs fostered compassion in her siblings.

All were dedicated to improving resources for the disabled.

Especially Eunice, who started day camps that evolved into the international Special Olympics.

Teddy worked hard on passing legislation to help the disabled. "Rosemary," he said, "taught us the worth of every human being."

The Jacksons

When Being Siblings
Is Your Job

The Jackson siblings got along well—so well that they actually felt sorry for only children. "We were encased in a very special bubble," remembered Janet Jackson, and they loved it.

In all, there were nine Jackson kids growing up in Gary, Indiana: Maureen (Reebie), Jackie, Tito, Jermaine, La Toya, Marlon, Michael, Randy, and Janet.

In the family's two-bedroom, one-bathroom house, the parents had one bedroom, while the girls slept on a sofa bed in the living room. The brothers slept in the other bedroom, in stacked bunk beds. "Your best friends are your brothers," their mom told them—and they actually were.

The cramped house overflowed with music. Their dad played guitar in a blues band during spare moments away from his two jobs, as a crane operator and a factory worker. Their mom taught them all the folk songs from her childhood.

"We sang constantly in the house," said Michael. "We sang group harmony while washing dishes" and finishing the rest of the chores on their long list.

Jackie, Jermaine, and Tito would borrow their dad's guitar and go off to harmonize together as a trio. Their stern father caught Tito playing the precious guitar and was about to punish him. Then he listened to the boy play and bought him his own guitar. Marlon joined up, playing the tambourine, while baby Michael flailed away on the bongos. More and more music burst out of the little house's four walls.

The siblings seldom sparred. "There was no fighting of any kind, not even in play," La Toya said later. "We worried about hurting one another's feelings, and if you know anything about kids, this is hardly typical."

In fact, the kids grew up going out of their way to avoid confrontation. "I was never forced out of my comfort zone," said La Toya. True, one brother or the other could be a "creep" or "a typically pesky brother"—Michael might call her Moonface (teasing her about her round face), or Jermaine might nab her dessert by breathing on it (knowing she wouldn't touch it). But such offenses were minor, and the good times far outweighed the bad. If she needed cheering up, Michael would go out and get a stack of magazines for her or a Three Stooges video to watch together. Tito even learned to use their mom's sewing machine and would make new clothes for her Barbie.

In their in-house boy band, Jermaine was the lead singer, until one day their mom noticed four-year-old Michael brilliantly imitating Jermaine in a sweet falsetto. "I loved his sound," Michael said of Jermaine later. "He showed me the way."

It was pretty obvious from the beginning that Michael Jackson was going to be the star. He says he was aware of his gift at age five, when he sang "Climb Ev'ry Mountain" in school and got a standing ovation.

Jermaine was okay with that. He was always Michael's role model and protector. He walked Michael to school, watched out for him during the day, passed his clothes on to him. Michael adored him: "He was funny and easygoing, and was constantly fooling around."

At first the boys loved competing and succeeding at sports. But their dad didn't want sports injuries interfering with their music, and soon they gave up every activity except music. Under the tight control of their dad, they practiced endlessly.

The first public performance of the Jackson Five, at a shopping center, was on Michael's seventh birthday (though, as Jehovah's Witnesses, the family didn't celebrate birthdays). It was a smash hit. Their mom made them matching outfits, and the brothers started playing gigs around town.

Michael morphed into a dancing machine, working out the moves for the whole group. With his dancing, charm, and soaring voice, he carried an unusual burden for a child, the group's success resting on his small sequined shoulders.

To his younger siblings, Michael thought of himself as "a big brother first and a dance teacher second." One day, as Randy was trying to copy his moves, Michael swooped in to save him from dancing right into a puddle.

Their dad's theme was "When you stick together, you are unbreakable." But none of the siblings remember him ever showing any sign of affection. His discipline went beyond tough love and into "Spare the rod, spoil the child."

"One glare was enough to make us wobble," recalled Jermaine.

"We were terrified of him," said Michael.

Despite his talent, Michael often bore the brunt of their dad's attention: "I would never get spanked during rehearsals or practice. But afterwards was when I got in trouble. . . . My father would rehearse with a belt in his hand. You couldn't mess up."

But under their dad's management, the brothers were a hit— these adorable, skillful child performers. Soon they were making records and traveling to play larger halls in distant cities, chauffeured by their dad in a VW van. Some places they played, like strip clubs, weren't particularly appropriate for kids, but the show would go on.

The brothers became so polished, they could perform well no matter what. Their dad, said Michael, taught them, "Never let the audience know if you are suffering, or if something's going wrong." Rules were strict. Grades had to be kept up, even with five shows a night, or the offender would be yanked off the road.

"It was exciting," said Michael, "but sometimes I'd be so tired I couldn't even see straight."

When their father wasn't watching, the boys found ways to have fun—they wrestled, had pillow fights and shaving cream wars, raced down hotel corridors, jumped on mattresses, made model airplanes, and played practical jokes with whoopee cushions, water balloons, itching powder. Michael was the biggest joker. If a brother fell asleep in the van with his mouth open, he would write something like "My breath smells" on a piece of paper and stick it to his lip.

Michael still idolized Jermaine. He always stood on Jermaine's right on stage. In hotels he always slept in the bed on the left. If Jermaine was chasing a girl, Michael would try to interfere and break them up.

"The diversity of my brothers' personalities," Michael said, "and the closeness we felt were what kept me going during those grueling days of constant touring. . . . Part of me wanted us to stay as we were—brothers who were also best friends."

Tito agreed: "I would like my children to be in a group like the Jackson Five, if they're willing to work hard enough to make themselves really good and if they can be as happy as we were."

They kept conversation light, about their dance moves, albums, basketball, girls. As Jermaine explained, "We were brothers first, artists second."

The brothers presented a united front except when fans mobbed them. If they faced scary situations trying to get to the van—"When it's time to run, it's every man for himself," said Jermaine.

By 1983, the brothers had sold more than a hundred million

records. They even had a Saturday-morning cartoon show based on the Jackson Five. Money was pouring in. Becoming famous and rich was disorienting, but brotherhood kept them focused.

It was a dream come true when the family moved from their two-bedroom house into a private estate near Los Angeles, a gigantic house with a pool, a basketball court, a private movie theater, groves of lemon and orange trees. In response to death threats and fan invasions, they had several guard dogs.

Inevitably, changes came. Reebie, Randy, La Toya, and Janet weren't content standing on the sidelines and started contributing to the group. It wasn't a boy band anymore but more of a family act, known as the Jacksons, still totally close-knit. La Toya recalled, appearing with her family "as the Jacksons was . . . one of the happiest times of my life. There's really nothing like a family working together."

And Michael kept soaring above and beyond. At twenty-one, he took charge of his own career, leaving the group and firing his dad, saying, "Mixing family and business can be a delicate situation." He felt Jermaine's absence: "When I did that first show without him . . . I felt totally naked on stage."

With hit after hit, he was a solo superstar, bringing joy to billions. His trademark sequined glove was a suggestion from Jackie, but his electric dance moves—like the moonwalk—were all his own. Michael became a groundbreaking artist, the first African American performer to appear on MTV, the most popular star in the world, the King of Pop.

"In most families," said La Toya, "that kind of individual attention would breed jealousy and rivalries, but not in the Jacksons." Everyone understood Michael's rare talent.

One by one, the siblings married and had children—all except Michael, who just kept evolving as a musician: "My wife is my music and I'm married to my craft." He did finally get married, to someone almost as famous as he was—Elvis Presley's daughter, Lisa Marie. He wanted to outdo his father and have eleven or twelve kids, but the marriage didn't last. From a second brief marriage, he had three children.

All the siblings continued their careers in various ways. Janet started writing her own songs at age nine, got her first record deal at sixteen, and went on to a stunning solo career as a pop star in her own right.

In 1984, on their last tour as the Jackson Five, the brothers performed fifty-five shows over five months. Michael didn't want to do it, "but my brothers wanted to do it and I did it for them. . . . It was a nice feeling, playing with my brothers again."

Through all the ups and downs, the siblings tried to stay close. "We still love each other's company," Michael said. At least once a month they had an official family day, when they played charades and Uno, watched movies, and caught up with each other.

In 2009, Michael died suddenly of cardiac arrest, at age fifty. There was hardly a place on the globe that hadn't been touched by his music, and the whole world mourned along with his family.

His memorial was watched on TV by one billion people, with millions trying to attend it in person. Janet spoke: "To you, Michael was an icon. To us, Michael was family. And he will forever live in all of our hearts."

The Jackson Five was the first child group to sell more than a million records.

They were also the first group of any age to start off with four straight number one hits.

They paved the way for several generations of boy bands (not necessarily brothers) . . .

from New Kids on the Block to One Direction.

Man in the Mirror

Among other examples of abusive behavior, the Jacksons' dad was always criticizing Michael's appearance, calling him Big Nose.

Perhaps this led to the cosmetic surgery he had as an adult. He admitted to at least two operations on his nose, but over the years his face changed so much that many believe he had more surgeries.

Some wondered if he was trying to look like Janet.

He would joke, "Me and Janet really are two different people."

Cars

One Jackson rule was that you had to be eighteen to have a car, and you had to buy your own.

Michael's first car was a Rolls-Royce.

He mainly used it to drive to his brothers' houses—he didn't really enjoy driving.

Breaking More Records

While on tour as a child, Michael was the one brother who spent nights reading books.

The Guinness Book of World Records was a favorite, and he was determined to get in it someday.

When his album *Thriller* became the biggest-selling record of all time, he made it into the record book.

Then he made it again as the pop star supporting the most charity organizations.

Stephen Colbert & His Ten Older Siblings

Lessons in Comedy
and Tragedy

JimmyEddieMaryBillyMargoTommyJayLuluPaulPeterStephen.
When he became a famous comedian and talk show host, Stephen Colbert made people laugh out loud at the chronological listing of his siblings' names. Eleven of them—and what pure joy it was to be the youngest.

His spot in the family definitely had perks. When he came home from the hospital in South Carolina, he was greeted as a cross between a new puppy and a live baby doll: "I was very loved," he said.

"They used to do little tricks with him," marveled the siblings' mother, Lorna. His sisters carried him around so much that it was a wonder he learned to walk.

Also, in their house, Lorna served dinner from the youngest to the oldest, so Stephen always got to eat first. "That way, I'd also be ready for seconds first," he said.

When he was a toddler, his older sisters woke him up at night to keep them company while they watched *The Tonight Show Starring Johnny Carson*. Did he get the show's jokes? No, but he'd laugh along anyway, just happy to be hanging out with his cool sisters.

"I always got a lot of attention. It became an addiction. I need attention," he admitted. He was a bit like a family mascot, and it ruled.

Whenever their doctor dad got home, the kids wrestled each other to make sure he felt welcome and pampered.

Was there a more concrete form of sibling rivalry in the Colbert family? Yes, but it took an unusual form, an art form. His siblings were always one-upping each other and finishing each other's sentences in clever ways. With verbal swordplay, they energized each other. Later, Stephen actually described his own comic style as a mash-up of his siblings' styles.

The family was a "humorocracy," he explained, "where the funniest person in the room is king." They were constantly trying to make the others fall on the floor laughing. Even their mom participated: "She'd trained to be an actress when she was younger," Stephen said, "and she would teach us to do stage falls by pretending to faint on the kitchen floor."

Stephen thought that his brother Jay was the funniest, and that *all* his siblings were funnier than he was: "I wasn't a particularly funny kid."

As proof, he points to the day he eavesdropped on his mother. She was warning his siblings that they *had* to listen to his stories, even though they complained that their little brother was boring: "And to this day I sort of feel like if I'm doing well with an audience, then Mom's gotten to them and said, 'You *listen* to him.'"

One of Lorna's rules was that "no fight between siblings could end without hugs and kisses." Another was that singing and

129

dancing were always appropriate. One final rule was to "never refuse a legitimate adventure."

The family attended Mass every week, although by the time Peter, the tenth Colbert, was born, they had to use two cars. Margo remembered a Sunday when they were driving away from church and Lorna saw someone hold up a sobbing little boy. "I remember Mom saying, 'Oh, that poor little boy . . . oh my gosh, that's *Paul*!'"

After that, Dr. Colbert counted noses whenever the family traveled together. The number of kids might have been right, but unfortunately they weren't necessarily all Colberts. One time, a sibling got left behind because one of the kids who had responded was a friend, not a Colbert. "After that, we had to answer by name," said Margo.

JimmyEddieMaryBillyMargoTommyJayLuluPaulPeterStephen.

Finally, they got a station wagon that could hold them all. After church they would go for Sunday drives. Their dad's preference was to visit Civil War battlefield sites, and he would bribe the siblings with the promise of ice cream. When they weren't too busy joking around, he would give them pop quizzes about nature or history.

Part of their father's job as dean of a medical school was to hire the best researchers and doctors, and at the dinner table, the kids would have to hold their own when Nobel Prize winners were dining with them. On those nights, making intelligent dinner conversation was more important than being funny.

Then, one day, all the funniness drained out of the Colbert family.

Stephen's father and two of his brothers were killed in a plane crash. The brothers—Peter (age eighteen) and Paul (age fifteen)—were the two closest to Stephen in age.

Suddenly, ten-year-old Stephen's life completely changed. He went from life in an overflowing house to living almost as an only child.

The whole family was crushed with grief. "We were all very family-oriented," said brother Eddie. "It was the only thing that mattered."

But the other siblings were mostly out of the house by then, off to school or on with their lives, and so it was just Stephen and his mother at home together for the next several lonely years.

Lorna encouraged the siblings to remain positive and move forward, to "put one foot in front of the other," to believe that "life [was] still good." But the death of her husband and two of her sons was almost too much to bear.

"The shades were down, and she wore a lot of black," said Stephen. "It was very quiet." He worked overtime to try to make her laugh. "I did my best to cheer my mom up," he said. "Mom and I used to joke that I raised my mom."

His own way of escaping grief was to start reading a book a day. Two of his older brothers were science fiction fans, so he lost himself in borrowed science fiction and fantasy novels, especially the works of J. R. R. Tolkien. He has an encyclopedic knowledge of the Lord of the Rings trilogy. He was also obsessed with fantasy role-playing games like Dungeons and Dragons. He would create characters based on the personalities of his siblings—and all would get killed off except Lulu, for some reason.

In sixth grade, he switched to a new school, where he was considered a nerd. "I was beaten up on a regular basis," he recalls.

In high school he started making jokes for people other than his siblings. He discovered a whole new audience. "The beginning of my junior year, nobody knew me at school. A year later, I was voted wittiest, and people were happy when I showed up at parties."

How, during that painful time, was he able to fine-tune his sense of humor? "Freud claimed that people don't develop a sense of humor until their sense of childhood happiness has vanished," he said. "I think comedians are in some way damaged."

He says that if he couldn't laugh, he would cry. "You know what I like about comedy? You can't laugh and be afraid at the same time—of anything. If you're laughing, I defy you to be afraid."

Making others laugh ruled even more than being the baby of the family. In his senior year he was voted class clown and got involved in local theater around Charleston. In college, he studied philosophy before switching to a theater major.

Starting his acting career, he observed that Southerners were often stereotyped as being less intelligent than other characters on television. He taught himself to suppress his Southern accent and imitate the speech of American news anchors.

He could be funny in any accent. After he delighted audiences on *The Daily Show* for years, his boss, Jon Stewart, thought he was so funny, he helped Stephen get his own TV show, *The Colbert Report*. Over the course of 1,500 episodes, his edgy political humor made audiences howl with the "truthiness" of what he had to say. Now he hosts another show, *The Late Show with Stephen Colbert*.

When not being funny on-screen, he teaches Sunday school, makes his kids laugh with silly stunts, cooks meals with them at their New Jersey house, and continues to hang out with his siblings.

Making a connection through humor is still meaningful to

them. Once, they were driving to the cemetery where their father, Peter, Paul, and their mother (who died in 2013, at age ninety-two) are buried, and his sister Mary made another sister, Margo, laugh so hard that she fell on the floor of the car snorting—"even in the midst of how we were feeling at that moment."

His surviving siblings may love to laugh, but they have jobs that don't sound particularly amusing. A few are in the military, and one ran for Congress. Others are doctors, lawyers, and professors.

The sibs have things in common. "I think my brothers and sisters are so much funnier than me," Stephen still insists. "When we are together as a family, I just listen to them—but I have stolen from them over the years."

They all love Charleston, where most of them live and where Stephen always takes his kids on vacation. Says Ed: the city is "a big hot cluster of Colberts." And all of them still adore their little brother.

Babies Are Funny

Babies in the family have to figure out how to get their share of attention.

They often discover that making the other family members laugh is the way to go.

Snagging the spotlight can become a lifelong quest.

Other Famous Comedians Who Were the Youngest

Jim Carrey, Whoopi Goldberg, Drew Carey,

Eddie Murphy, Billy Crystal,

Rosie O'Donnell, Steve Martin,

Ellen DeGeneres, and Charlie Chaplin.

What Would Freud Say?

Sigmund Freud, father of modern psychology, had something to say about almost everything people do.

He saw sibling rivalry as a very real, potentially deadly thing: "A small child does not necessarily love his brothers and sisters. . . .

"There is no doubt that he hates them as his competitors"—and may hate them all his life.

(Freud, as it happens, was the oldest of eight and did his best to pretend he was an only child.)

Five Signs You're the Youngest Child

1. You wear a lot of hand-me-down clothes.

2. You started watching R-rated movies earlier than your peers.

3. You know more swear words than most of your peers.
4. You get privileges that your older siblings had to fight for.

5. You're secretly sure that you're the most loved.

Peyton & Eli Manning

Gentlemen—Except on the Football Field

Peyton Manning and Eli Manning are professional football superstars, smashing and thrashing records all over the place. But the source of strength and inspiration for both of them?

A third brother, their older one, Cooper Manning.

As they grew up in New Orleans, Louisiana, all three brothers learned the game by watching their father. He was yet *another* famous professional football player—Archie Manning. (Truly, the Mannings are football's royal family.)

The boys started as tiny football-playing toddlers on the rug in their living room, conveniently shaped like a football field. On rainy days they played a game they called Amazing Catches. Archie would throw balls from the porch, and they adored it, even if catching a ball meant crawling in the mud to get it.

Cooper invented the Ten Questions game, thinking of an athlete and giving the others ten chances to guess who it was.

While Archie was in the locker room, Peyton and Cooper would amuse themselves by making footballs out of bunches of athletic wrapping tape and tossing them back and forth, pretending they were scoring big plays.

"Because we were two years apart, we fought a lot," Cooper admitted. He wouldn't allow *other* kids to pick on Peyton, but, in typical big-brother fashion, "I was allowed to pick on him because he was my brother, so it worked out nicely."

Peyton was forced to agree: "From childhood we were competitive to the extreme. We'd fight, I think mainly so that he could get the satisfaction of making me cry." A fight might start with a simple insult, like "Wimp!"—and explode from there.

Or, to be extra annoying, Cooper would go in Peyton's room and mess everything up, take the phone off the hook, pull his covers off his bed. A bit of sibling devilry—Cooper was a slob, while Peyton was a neatnik.

After games, Archie would have the boys compete to give him the best massage on his sore muscles. But he opposed competing to the point of fighting. "You ought to be best friends," he would stress. "You don't know how lucky you are, having a brother."

So they mostly looked out for each other. To keep Peyton from getting totally demoralized, Cooper started letting him win a few of their one-on-one basketball games. In time, the brothers forged a special bond on the football field.

One year they got to play on the same team—"one of the best years I've ever had," said Peyton, as they were able to communicate with their own unique set of hand signals. Cooper treasured being on the field with his brother: "You're on the same genetic wavelength. You know each other's every move. And you've been living in the same house together all your lives. How could you beat that?"

Competing with Cooper made Peyton try harder and become better. "Beating his brother," noticed Archie, "was more than just a challenge, it was a crusade." His big brother showed him the way, said Peyton: "Cooper was my goad, and though he was a pain in the butt a lot of the time, he is now my very best friend."

Typical older brothers, they both felt that the youngest, Eli, got away with murder. The first word little Eli said was "ball," and he slept with a football in his crib. He had trouble learning to read at first and was almost held back but, with tutoring, caught up.

Cooper behaved less like a competitor and more like a big brother now because Eli was so much younger. And Peyton acted almost as a second father to Eli because Archie had demanding football games and practices during much of Eli's childhood. Peyton would teach him things in his own way, pinning Eli down to test him on football facts, playfully punching him if he got an answer wrong. Despite Peyton's unusual methods, Eli reveled in sports: "Growing up, we played every sport. Whatever season it was in, we were outside." During rare moments inside, they watched movies or *Seinfeld* episodes together.

Like many little brothers, Eli did sometimes feel like the "tagalong"—insecure, never quite sure if his brothers genuinely liked having him around. Or were they being punished by their parents and forced to hang out with him?

Groomed to be Southern gentlemen, the brothers went to an academic school, not one for jocks. Said Archie: "We tried to raise kids just like other parents raised their kids." Why they were all so talented, he said, "I can't explain." He wanted his sons to play for the fun of it, to be good people as well as good players. He and his wife had breakfast with their sons every morning and held weekly family meetings as well. They tried not to be pushy stage parents, just supportive, attending some 950 games over the years.

There was one notable lapse in the Manning manners, when twelve-year-old Peyton told his coach that he didn't know what he was doing. That night Archie drove Peyton over to the coach's house and made him apologize.

And at one point Mrs. Manning was heard to yell, "I'm *tired* of washing jockstraps!"

But then one brother fell behind. A star player in high school, Cooper planned to play football at the University of Mississippi. But he began

having problems on the field, uncharacteristically dropping passes. Alarmed, his coaches and parents took him to the doctor, to see if there was a medical cause for this physical change. He was diagnosed with spinal stenosis, a narrowing of the spine and pinching of the nerves, something usually seen only in elderly people. It was a serious condition that ended his playing career.

Cooper refused to feel sorry for himself. He said he's never had a "Why me?" personality and even thinks he was better equipped to deal with the setback than Peyton or Eli might have been: "Maybe the bad thing happened to the right guy."

So Cooper transformed himself into his brothers' number one cheerleader, always offering encouragement and advice, urging them on, and telling Peyton: "I'll be playing my dreams through you."

The brothers soared, playing college rivals, playing each other. Eli's favorite moments were when he could beat Peyton: "You beat your big brother in anything . . . it was a big step."

In college, within three years, Peyton earned a degree in speech communication and excelled academically. He was a number one draft pick and went on to a stellar career in the NFL. He was the starting quarterback for the Indianapolis Colts for fourteen exciting years, winning one Super Bowl, then led his next team, the Denver Broncos, to a Super Bowl win in the last game of his career. He became one of the most famous athletes in the United States, one of the greatest quarterbacks of all time, and was a five-time winner of the NFL Most Valuable Player award. As a reward for his excellence, he earned record amounts, in 2011 signing a five-year, $90 million contract.

Peyton was serious and focused on the field, though he usually appeared to be having more fun than Eli.

Peyton once wrote in his brother's yearbook: "Watch out, world, he's the best one." The pressure! Though Eli claimed to feel "honored, not pressured" by Peyton's reputation, it was hard. Would he be as good as Peyton—better? Worse? On a bad day, people sometimes wondered cruelly if he was adopted. But after a

big win: "It is hard to explain what that feeling is. You don't know whether to scream or cry or yell. You don't know what to do."

Eli graduated with high grades and a degree in marketing from the University of Mississippi. Like his older brother, Eli was a number one draft pick. As the starting quarterback for the New York Giants, he led them to two Super Bowl victories and broke numerous records. A two-time MVP, he signed a four-year, $84 million extension with his team in 2015.

Whenever Peyton is asked who his favorite player is, he loyally says, "My little brother." During rare joint interviews, Peyton usually answers all the questions, even the ones directed at his brother. On camera they have been caught in unrehearsed moments of bickering, jabbing, poking, pushing, and even kicking—but all in good fun, or so they say.

Their affection is genuine: "It's great that you have a brother and a best friend," said Eli, "and a guy who's also the NFL MVP. . . . You can talk about certain things and he knows exactly what you're talking about and sometimes he doesn't have to give advice, it just gives you someone to listen to."

The brothers also compete with each other in their charity work. Peyton started his own charity, the PeyBack Foundation. Its mission is to help disadvantaged kids in Louisiana, Tennessee, and Indiana. He's also worked on behalf of the Special Olympics, the Boys & Girls Clubs of America, and foster children—and has a children's hospital named for him.

Eli has a children's hospital named for him too. He contributes to a wide range of causes, like Guiding Eyes, a nonprofit guide-dog school serving the visually impaired, as well as children on the autism spectrum, around the world. After the devastation of Hurricane Katrina, Peyton and Eli rented a plane, loaded it with water, Gatorade, and baby formula, and flew to New Orleans to help.

During the summers, the three brothers and their dad run the Manning Passing Academy, an intensive camp that coaches high schoolers in four different football positions.

They still enjoy each other's company, though these days it's usually a challenge to get the brothers' schedules to mesh. As Peyton says, "I miss the chances to just hang out like when we were kids." But somehow they still manage to meet up to golf, hunt, travel, tell old stories, recite quotes from movies and episodes of *Seinfeld* . . . and talk football.

Extra Large

Both Peyton and Eli weighed more than 12 pounds at birth.

Now one weighs 225 pounds, and the other 230.

The Importance of Cooper

To this day Cooper speaks to his brothers on the phone several times a week. "He's still my best friend," Peyton says. "It's just nice to be able to call him and talk to him about anything."

The oldest Manning hosts his own show, *The Manning Hour*, on Fox Sports and is a partner in an energy investment firm.

Pop Go the Mannings

Peyton has been named the NFL personality most likely to become a Jedi knight.

Both Peyton and Eli have hosted *Saturday Night Live*.

All three brothers guest-voiced on an episode of *The Simpsons* called "O Brother, Where Bart Thou?" Bart is dreaming of having a baby brother and sees such famous brothers as the Marx Brothers, the Blues Brothers, the Wright brothers—and the Manning brothers.

Serena & Venus Williams

"We Can Be Sisters Later"

Today Venus and Serena Williams are the powerhouse goddesses of tennis, multimillionaire sisters living the life.

It wasn't always this way. They grew up in Compton, California, a poor neighborhood notorious for gang violence at that time. The first tennis court they played on was made of cracked asphalt littered with broken glass, sprouting weeds, trash, and drug gear. Before they were trained in tennis, they already knew to drop to the ground on the court when gunshots rang out.

Their neighbors knew them as the little girls always playing tennis at the public park, so jazzed to play that they would do cartwheels and handsprings on the way there. Venus would cry when it was time to leave. Said Serena: "I still miss the ice cream trucks" that patrolled the park.

According to family legend, their dad determined that these two daughters would be tennis superstars two years before Venus was born.

Sounds impossible, but he came up with a master plan to coach them, organizing their daily routines, schooling, and diets around their future careers as tennis stars. Their mom (who ran track and played tennis and several other sports) was fully on board with getting them motivated. She remembers, "They weren't allowed to say C-A-N'-T." The sisters also took boxing, ballet, and tae kwon do.

Sometimes Serena did have to be bribed with curly french fries to do her best at practice. But by nine, she *hated* to lose.

Said Venus: "We were just young and playing hours of tennis, having fun, reaching for the dream."

Tennis was a mostly white world, and their dad knew that every move they made would be greeted with controversy. He toughened them up by paying kids from the local schools to surround the courts while Venus and Serena practiced. "I had the kids call them every curse word in the English language," he said, including the n-word. They needed to be on their guard against racism but still able to shut it out and focus on their game. Counting on each other and their family would get them through it.

The sisters were super close. Older sister Venus walked Serena to kindergarten, gave her lunch money when she forgot it, even let her have a trophy if Serena admired it. Serena wanted everything Venus had, like guitar lessons and the same meals. Their mom would force Serena to order first at restaurants or else she would just get whatever Venus was having.

"I have the world's best big sister," Serena swore. At times they almost blended together, creating a weird sort of identity crisis. Serena later said, "I was Venus. . . . There were two Venus Williamses in the Williams family. . . . It was really tough for me to finally stop being Venus and become the person who I am, Serena."

Venus, as always, was there to help. "Serena knows exactly what she wants in life. And if she doesn't know, then I help her to know." Serena called her a "benevolent bodyguard."

Venus and Serena had three older sisters—Yetunde, Isha, and Lyndrea—from their mom's first marriage. All five Williams sisters shared a bedroom with two sets of bunk beds.

Right—five sisters, four beds.

Instead of feeling left out, Serena felt special. Each night she would crawl into bed with a different sister. "I felt like I belonged everywhere. It was empowering."

They loved to dress her up and play with her like a doll. One sister said, "All of us spoil Serena, including Serena, if it's possible." One of Serena's hobbies, actually, was looking in a mirror: "I was the princess. I was everyone's pet. Looking back, I think I was more like a pest, but my sisters let me get away with everything!"

Serena could be more than a pest. Once, she reportedly cut off a sister's braids. And when they were all given pretty piggy banks and hers broke, she broke all of her sisters' banks too. "Cute cuts you a lot of slack," she said slyly.

But the sisterhood stayed strong. As Yetunde, the oldest, said, "They're my sisters. I mean, we argue. We have disagreements. It's no different."

In the four years before Venus and Serena turned pro, they practiced six hours a day, six days a week. Each was brought up to believe she would someday be number one in the world. According to Serena,

156

"Whatever my potential is, I want to reach it—now. And if I do, I see Venus as my biggest competition."

Venus plays with grace and little emotion. Serena is all grunts and glares and has been known to break rackets and yell. Different styles, but both winners.

Each Williams sister rocked the tennis world, breaking all kinds of records, every which way. Venus won four Olympic gold medals and on three separate occasions was ranked the number one player in women's singles tennis. She is credited with changing the women's game and ushering in a new, modern era of power and athleticism.

She also ushered in Serena: "You better believe it. Venus's success was a powerful motivator for me."

Serena is ranked by many as simply the greatest female tennis player of all time. She also won four Olympic gold medals and was ranked the number one player in women's singles tennis six times. She's extra famous for the "Serena Slam"—achieving the Grand Slam, or winning all four of the major tennis tournaments in one year, not once but *twice*. In 2016, Serena, at thirty-four, was still the world's number one women's tennis player, and Venus, at thirty-five, was number eleven. In 2017, Serena made history by winning her twenty-third grand slam, beating her sister, among others.

They've gone up against each other in some thirty matches, and that's where the sisterly bond has been tested. Somehow they've learned to leave the mental baggage of sisterhood behind when they play, disconnecting their emotions.

Oh, really?

Serena tries to compartmentalize: "I love her dearly (she's my best friend!), but that gets tossed while we're playing. . . . She feels the same way. We tell each other we can be sisters later." Using her brain in this complicated way adds another level of difficulty to the game.

The only place Serena doesn't get pampered by her sister is on the court. When Venus is winning: "I try not to look at her because I might start feeling bad. I want the best for her. I love her so much."

And apparently there is such a thing as winner's remorse. If Venus wins, she feels apologetic, sort of: "It wasn't fun eliminating my little sister, but I have to be tough. After the match, I said, 'I'm sorry I had to take you out.' . . . I really wouldn't want to lose. But that's the only person I would be happy losing to."

Serena *tries* to use the same not-looking technique: "I don't look at Venus on the court. I can't," she said. "If I am winning, I might feel sorry for her. If I'm losing, I will want to knock her out." Ouch!

Serena envisions Venus as just another opponent—one to beat: "I have this mean, steely look when I play, so I'll just stare down at my opponent if our eyes happen to meet. No big thing. But with V, I worry I'll smile or break out laughing, so it's better

158

not to look and maybe cut the tension. Better to let it build and tighten and try to use it to my advantage."

Serena tends to win, but it's always a nail-biter. Their mom is in the worst pickle of all: "I can't root for either one because I don't want either one to get mad at me . . . especially Serena. Venus will be able to handle it, but Serena, no."

Together, the Williams sisters can take credit for launching a new era of power tennis for women. Their success also led to many more African Americans taking up the sport.

Serena does most of the talking. "It's hard and lonely at the top," she observed. "You're a target when you're number one. Everyone wants to beat you. Everyone talks behind your back, and you get a lot more criticism."

In 2003, when Yetunde was killed in a drive-by shooting near the courts where the sisters once practiced, the family issued a statement: "Our grief is overwhelming, and this is the saddest day of our lives." The loss was so harsh that some wondered if the two sisters would quit tennis. But as Serena put it, "And now she was gone, and the four

of us would have to take turns in her number one spot, filling the spaces where she had been."

Sisterhood always comes to their rescue. It was Venus who made Serena go to the hospital when her leg swelled up because of a pulmonary embolism. Later she got Serena to college and signed her up for classes. Now it is Serena who consoles Venus as she confronts a disorder of the immune system that threatens her career. Both have had many injuries. Serena's worst didn't even happen while playing tennis: she messed up her knee while dancing in high heels.

The sisters never stop percolating with new ideas. Venus has a degree in fashion design and another in business, and speaks three languages. Serena loves Paris and spends much of her time there. The two of them became part owners of the Miami Dolphins, the first African American women to own an NFL franchise.

Both play guitar—Serena electric, and Venus acoustic. Serena drives a Rolls-Royce, while Venus jokes, "Uh, I get rides." They sponsor numerous philanthropic activities, touring Africa to promote tennis among African women and funding schools there, insisting that all-boys schools have to start including girls, who should make up at least 40 percent of the student body.

Another sister said they all gossip with each other all the time: "We talk about life issues, about men, about world issues, you know, just everything. . . . I think it is one of the greatest things in the world to have sisters. . . . There's nothing like it."

Even now, in their thirties and millionaires many times over, the two sisters are far from being tired of each other. They lived together for many years in a Florida mansion in a gated community, with three dogs, just down the road from the ten-acre estate they bought for their family. Venus decorated their place with marble floors and gigantic crystal chandeliers. When Serena won the 2017 Australian Open, she was two months' pregnant. That September, she had a baby girl, Alexis Olympia. After she marries her fiancé, she'll be moving to San Francisco—with plenty of visits back to Florida.

They live like rock stars—with rock-star problems such as security issues and a lack of privacy. But solutions to such problems, as with any others, are always to be found in the tie of sisterhood.

What Are the Odds?

The notion of two top professionals emerging from the same family to compete against each other is so rare that it has been described as being "as improbable as one set of parents raising Picasso and Monet."

The Manning brothers are a similar oddity, but they haven't competed head-to-head as much as the Williams sisters have.

Small World

The Williams sisters actually know the Manning brothers and have held Oreo-eating contests with them.

A Win for Women

In the famed Battle of the Sexes in 1973, Billie Jean King beat Bobby Riggs and won $100,000 and respect for women tennis players.

But equal pay for women players didn't come until 2007, after Venus fought hard on and off the court to win true equality.

"Somewhere in the world a little girl is dreaming of holding a giant trophy in her hands and being viewed as an equal to boys who have similar dreams," she said.

Don't Mess with Serena's Phone

In 2015, while eating out, Serena had her cell phone stolen.

Not one to take these things lightly, she chased the thief down: "Fight for what's right," she posted afterward.

"Stand for what you believe in! Be a superhero! When I got back into the restaurant I received a standing ovation.

"I was proud. I just showed every man in there I can stand up to bullies and other men. It was a win for the ladies!"

What Is It About All-Girl Families?

Do girls from sisters-only families feel more empowered to succeed?

Some studies show that parents of all-girl families are more likely to be in favor of gender equality—so they're more likely to make sure their daughters get fair treatment.

One study shows that having an older sister tends to make younger sisters more competitive . . .

. . . which could explain their great accomplishments.

Princes William & Harry

An Heir and a Spare

Perhaps no royal siblings in history have had less privacy than British princes William and Harry. Also known as the Heir and the Spare, one will eventually inherit the throne and become king, with the other, two years younger, in the line of succession after him.

When Elizabeth II, the queen of England, is your grandma—sorry, *grandmother*, because that's how formal and stuffy she is—you live in a fishbowl. As a lifestyle, living in a fishbowl is creepy, distressing, and dangerous. Many a time the two princes must have wished they could borrow invisibility cloaks from Harry Potter.

With newspapers in England (much more intrusive than they

are here) tapping the palace phones and spying on them, they grew up like bugs under a microscope. A new haircut or tooth would *immediately* appear in the papers. Reporters revealed that William's parents called him Wombat—and also Your Royal Nightmare. Apparently he had a bad case of sibling-rivalry tantrums after Harry was born.

At seven, William reportedly told his mother that he wanted to grow up to be a police officer so that he could protect her. Harry jumped in to say, "Oh, no, you can't. You've got to be king." This was true—already he was having weekly lunch dates with the queen to get some pointers.

As they grew up, Harry (the Spare) was allowed to be a bit goofier. When he knew reporters were spying from the bushes, he urged his friends to moon them. In class he thought it was hilarious to silently hide behind curtains while the teacher repeatedly called his name for attendance. Or he'd balance a book on the top of a door so that it fell when the teacher entered the classroom. When Queen Elizabeth got her first cell phone, he programmed her message to say, "Hey, wassup? This is Liz."

In the British royal family, child rearing is formal, often left to nannies and tutors. But the boys' mother—Princess Diana, one of the most famous women in the world—was hands-on. She showered them with affection, protected them from cameras as much as she could, and got them interested in her causes—helping the victims of land mines, the homeless, and AIDS patients.

She wanted her boys to have broader experience than typical royal children have—life isn't all polo playing and foxhunting (though both boys were still "blooded" at fourteen—smeared with the blood of their first killed animal). She took them to Walt Disney World and fast-food restaurants as well as AIDS clinics, children's hospitals, and shelters for the homeless.

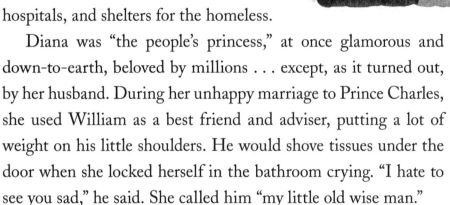

Diana was "the people's princess," at once glamorous and down-to-earth, beloved by millions . . . except, as it turned out, by her husband. During her unhappy marriage to Prince Charles, she used William as a best friend and adviser, putting a lot of weight on his little shoulders. He would shove tissues under the door when she locked herself in the bathroom crying. "I hate to see you sad," he said. She called him "my little old wise man."

Their parents' bitter separation and divorce made for juicy headlines but intense embarrassment for the boys, then age fourteen and eleven. They were never more relieved to be brothers. "We've got each other to talk to," said Harry. "We are both very grateful that, you know, each of us was there as a shoulder to cry on if we needed to."

The boys were lucky to get a break from the unwanted

attention when they were away at boarding school. But even when they were apart, the boys stayed in constant contact with their mom. In one phone call, in 1997, fifteen-year-old Will asked her for advice about how to keep twelve-year-old Harry from being overshadowed by him at school.

This turned out to be the last conversation they ever had. The next day, Diana was being chased by aggressive photographers in Paris when her car smashed into a concrete pillar.

Their mom was dead at thirty-six. At her funeral, the white envelope on the coffin, labeled "Mummy" in Harry's writing, broke the world's heart.

Their grief was intensified when an endless series of tell-all books and articles appeared, written by people Diana knew and trusted. It was nearly impossible for the brothers to move on when the world was still obsessed with their mom.

Any news about these beloved princes was worth a lot of money. A reporter was even jailed for hacking into their private voice-mail boxes, and newspapers hired private investigators to follow them everywhere. The boys had no idea whom to trust except each other.

Once again, they helped each other get through it all: "It's amazing how close we've become," said Harry. "We can talk about *anything*."

When William started college, the royal family made a deal: the press would leave him alone to study, and in exchange, William would give them regular updates about his life.

But right off the bat, the boys' own uncle, Prince Edward, broke the rule. He sent in a camera crew to cover William's first few days at school so that he could make a documentary. William was outraged by his uncle's betrayal. Even worse, he soon learned that his dad had bugged his rooms so that he could listen to everything William ever did or said, believing it necessary to protect his son's safety (though his college firmly denies this happened).

Every member of the royal family is watched around the clock by the royal protection service and, sometimes, foreign powers. They can have no secrets. All conversations are recorded. They wear electronic tags around their necks in case something happens to them.

While in college the brothers were always accompanied by two bodyguards protecting them from potential assassins, antimonarchists, people against foxhunting, all sorts who opposed British rule. The buildings they lived in needed to have the windows and doors replaced with bulletproof glass and bombproof doors.

Their bodyguards would *try* to give them a zone of privacy, but—really?

"I feel kind of sorry for the dude," said one of William's classmates.

The brothers tried to make light of their predicament. William, when asked if they lived a normal life, pointed to Harry: "You may be abnormal. I'm pretty normal." Harry responded more sincerely, "No, I don't know. He enjoys himself more than people think. You know, he works very hard. He's definitely the more intelligent one of the two of us."

William tried to be normal by singing Beatles songs at karaoke bars, dancing wildly, holding burping competitions with chums. But reminders were everywhere. When the brothers did go out to clubs, they paid their way with "grannies." British paper money has the queen's face on the bills, and the boys called them pink, blue, or brown grannies, depending on their value.

William went to great lengths not to waste his "gap year," taking twelve months off before starting his university studies, wanting to follow in Diana's footsteps. He did good deeds, worked on English dairy farms, visited Africa, took part in British army training exercises in Belize. When he spent ten weeks teaching children in Chile, he lived with young teachers, sharing in the cleaning of toilets and the other household chores, spending his spare time as the guest radio jockey for the local radio station.

In college he specialized in art history and geography, then served more than seven years in military service doing helicopter search-and-rescue operations.

Harry, still more of a goofball, took not one but two gap years. But he put them to good use, working on a cattle farm in

Australia and helping orphans in a small African country. He spent ten years as an officer in the military, serving two tours in Afghanistan during the war.

At one point, the two brothers lived together for six months while they shared a cottage off base. Mistake. "The first time and the *last* time, I can assure you of that," said Harry, even though it was William complaining about Harry's snoring and general messiness. . . .

With most women in England eager to wed a royal heart-throb, the brothers took it slow when it came to romance. The very eligible William finally married Kate Middleton in a wedding that cost $30 million (the best man was, of course, Harry). Instead of wedding gifts, Will and Kate asked well-wishers to donate money to charities supporting war veterans, conservation, and young people.

The future king started his married life in the most remote corner of England he could find. Surrounded by the tightest security systems money can buy, his expanding family still gets invaded by the media. In 2015, the palace issued a letter begging the press to stop harassing and publishing photos of the new royal siblings, Prince George and Princess Charlotte.

Harry pops around to see them whenever he has a chance and, like a typical little brother, scrounges food. When William is off on royal business, or when Kate needs a laugh break, she calls Harry.

The brothers always seem like the best of friends, even when Harry is moaning about how boring he thinks Will is now that he has two little ones running around. Or teasing him about his thinning hair.

Only one topic gets them quarreling: rugby. Will is a patron of the Welsh Rugby Union, while Harry supports the English team.

The older William and Harry get, the more selfless they seem to be. For years Will was a pilot for the East Anglian Air Ambulance service, donating his entire salary to charity. He has taken on more royal duties, including awareness of mental health problems. Harry recently retired

from the military but continues to work with veterans and over-sees charities, including one for AIDS sufferers. Harry has also created the Invictus Games—an international sporting event meant to shine a spotlight on the sacrifices made by wounded war veterans and to celebrate their triumph over adversity. He is eager to be seen as more than "the Spare."

William is helping the monarchy enter the modern age by speaking out against homophobia, a normally taboo topic for royals. He has taken part in workshops on bullying and homophobia in schools, working out ways to prevent anti-LGBT bullying and cyberbullying.

William tries to be philosophical about coping with his immense fame: "You just let it wash over you, you know? I'm bigger than that. . . . At the end of the day, neither of us care much about images. We just—we're ourselves."

As for a more concrete way of coping, the only time William and Harry can feel normal and anonymous is when wearing motorcycle helmets. No wonder, then, that they're both enthusiastic motorcyclists.

Given their permanent state of sibling royalty, William and Harry are resigned to being famous every day of their lives, in the news constantly, doing ceremonial things. Their privacy will always be invaded . . . as this chapter demonstrates perfectly.

The Complexities of Being a Royal

William's full title is His Royal Highness Prince William Arthur Philip Louis, Duke of Cambridge, Earl of Strathearn, Baron Carrickfergus, Royal Knight Companion of the Most Noble Order of the Garter, Knight of the Most Ancient and Most Noble Order of the Thistle, Personal Aide-de-Camp to Her Majesty The Queen.

The Man Everyone Wants to Marry

Until his engagement to American Meghan Markle, Harry was the world's most eligible bachelor. He is sixth in line to the throne, after his father, William, and William's children, George, Charlotte, and the new baby on the way.

Money, Not Everything

Each member of the British royal family is worth untold millions.

What Christmas gifts do you give to people who have everything?

They make a joke out of it by laying out each person's gifts in piles on tables . . .

leather toilet seats, ugly teapots—the cheapest, tackiest presents they can find.

Morbid

Both princes have been asked to plan their own funerals, to make sure their wishes get carried out.

Queen Elizabeth II is the longest-reigning monarch in English history!

But why should she serve her country forever when she could be romping with her four corgis?

She's supposed to pass the throne to her son, Prince Charles. But rumors are flying.

Might she skip Charles and hand her crown directly to Prince William instead? Will he be the next king of England?

Demi Lovato & Madison De La Garza

Bullies, Beware
the Big Sister

Pop star Demi Lovato knows all too well what it's like to be bullied. And, if she can help it, no one is ever going to bully her nine-years-younger half sister, Madison De La Garza.

Demi began her life as a star early—singing, acting, competing in beauty pageants. Music was everywhere—her older sister Dallas was a singer and an actress, and their mother was a country-music singer. The family, later joined by Madison, was close-knit, eating dinner together and talking about their day, watching movies, visiting Disneyland.

At age five, Demi sang *Titanic*'s "My Heart Will Go On" in the kindergarten talent show, wowing everyone. She failed her first audition for TV because she couldn't read yet. But soon she was a regular on the show *Barney & Friends*. She worked on several shows with the Disney Channel and became the star of her own show, *Sonny with a Chance*.

As a child star, Demi worked harder than most adults, with hardly any time off. She soared to the top as one of the richest teens in America. On her eighteenth birthday, she treated her family to a large house in Los Angeles.

She started writing her own songs in seventh grade—

hundreds of songs. "It's kind of like therapy for me," she said, a way to address her problems. "I was writing seven songs in one night and I'd be up until five-thirty in the morning."

And Demi did have problems: bullies, jealous of her stunning success. Bullying was a huge issue for her at school. Mean girls called her fat and even started a "We Hate Demi" petition. It was ugly, and it hurt.

At the time she blamed herself. If she was "fat," she decided, "that's the reason I don't have any friends." So she stopped eating. She lost thirty pounds, dropping down to an unhealthy weight. "I'd be lying if I said there weren't days where I just want to stay in bed all day because I'm ashamed of my body. It's a struggle I'll probably have to deal with for the rest of my life."

The bullying got so bad that she decided to be homeschooled. She received her high school diploma in 2009.

But by then, she'd fallen into self-destructive patterns. Stories flew about bouts with eating disorders, self-harm, substance-abuse problems.

In a rehearsal, she hit one of her backup dancers. That and other incidents made her realize she needed help. So did her family, who held a meeting to show their support: "My mom specifically said, 'You know, we're going to move back to Texas and you're not going to be able to be around your little sister.'"

That was a jolt. Madison was precious to her: "I have a little sister whom I love with all my heart. . . . I would really be thinking about how my own actions might influence my little sister in her life. If I'm doing drugs in front of her, she's going to think that's OK."

The very real threat of not being able to see Madison because she was providing such a terrible example was what woke Demi up and motivated her to change. As she got professional help, she was diagnosed with bipolar disorder, which she now manages with medication, and her family is closer and stronger than ever.

Being a role model for Madison became more important than cravings: "We have to be conscious and mindful of all the things that we do and say knowing that younger generations are looking up to us."

Out of a desire to help others, Demi made a brave and deliberate decision to go public with her journey: "If I can just change one life by this message by saying don't go there—then I'm done." In talking so openly about her personal experiences, she has become a role model for many besides Madison.

She speaks out against bullying, among other issues, and projects a strong message of body acceptance and body positivity. While becoming ever more successful as a star with an incredible voice, she supports many charities, campaigns for lawmakers to make mental health a top priority, and is a fierce advocate for the LGBT community: "There are people whose voices aren't being heard, and I want to use my voice to speak up for them."

Throughout her struggle, she saw her sister as her guiding

light: "My sister Madison and I are always together. I can't pick one moment. I love being with her . . . she's so much fun and so funny. I am always quoting her."

She even uses Madison for career advice, trying out new dance moves in front of her to make sure they're appropriate for her younger fans: "So I performed them for my younger sister and asked if they were too much. She said they were fine, so they stayed in."

Only one thing drives her crazy (a typical big-sister complaint): Madison always playing with her makeup.

But Madison had her own career to start, and makeup was a part of it. She spent four years starring as Juanita Solis on the hit series *Desperate Housewives* and went on to appear in movies and other TV series.

But she too faced some cruel bullying, not in person but online. Starting when she was only six years old, Twitter trolls were labeling her "fat," "ugly," and even a "slut."

When Madison posted a photo of herself cooking in the kitchen with Demi, negative comments popped up. People started making fun of the way she looked, saying horrible things about her back. (In fact, Madison has scoliosis, a sideways curvature of the spine.)

Naturally, Madison was devastated: "No matter how strong you are, repetition inevitably takes its toll on you. At an extremely young age, I started to think maybe the cruel voices were right. Their opinions turned into my insecurity—and suddenly I was aware of every meal, every outfit, every post on social media."

It was Demi to the rescue, in a major case of sibling chivalry. Bullying her sister? Don't even think about it.

First she tried to help Madison

186

cope with her insecurities: "Like Demi told me, 'At the end of the day, what others say about you doesn't matter. What matters is how you cope with it and how you come out on the other side.'" Demi put all her effort into bolstering her sister's self-esteem, saying, "You are the only person who has to love you. After all, you only get one body—other people's opinions shouldn't interfere with the love you have for it."

Then Demi went on the attack, slamming and direct-messaging the trolls: "For anyone telling me to 'chill' . . . the impact bullies have over the internet can lead people to suicide. I can handle [it]. But do NOT [mess] with my baby sister."

Demi kept on roaring: "I'm all for peace and spreading love UNTIL you go after a 12 YEAR OLD who did NOTHING to you. So disappointed that after all the conversation about cyber bullying in this world that people would continue to do this to others. @Maddielovesyou1 you are BEAUTIFUL and the most precious little angel in my life and I will always protect you."

Take that, bullies. Who *wouldn't* want to have such a warrior big sister?

Madison was a little embarrassed but grateful: "Sometimes I wish she wouldn't give people attention—I've learned not to—but when people hate on me, she can't really hold back. She's strong and she's a free spirit, and that's what I love about her."

Since then, even when she's on the road, Demi encourages her sister to call her as much as possible: "I want her to come to me with things. I just let her know that I'm always there for her, whether I'm on the other side of the world or I'm next door."

Now that Demi is in her twenties and Madison is in her teens, the sisters are closer than ever. Demi is surely going to help with Madison's ambitious career plans—besides continuing with her acting, she wants to produce, direct, write, and do special-effects makeup. Madison will surely support Demi as she talks about working less on her music and more charity work.

The two text constantly, with Demi trying to make her sister laugh: "Whenever she sees a funny tweet, she'll screenshot it and send it to our family group message. My phone is constantly going off just from that."

But best of all is when Demi is home: "Our relationship is just like any sisters'. We get fro-yo and watch the ID [Investigation Discovery] channel—we're obsessed—and we talk about anything and everything. I know I can trust her with it all."

It's hard to tell who needs whom more because, as Demi points out, Madison does a lot for her: "When I was younger, I needed someone in the spotlight to idolize, who stood for positivity and light and happiness, and wanted to change the world.

And because I didn't have that, I realized I want to do that, if only for my . . . little sister."

Big sister, little sister, BFFs. As Demi says, "Soak up the love of your family today. Love them for everything they are and aren't."

How to Bounce Back

Proving that she's bounced back from being bullied on social media . . .

Madison has her own YouTube channel, Mad de la Garza.

Who Is Poot Lovato?

Poot is an Internet meme created in 2015 out of an awkward picture of Demi.

Someone snarky found a photo of Demi at a weird angle and labeled it Demi's imaginary twin sister:

"She was locked in a basement her whole life. This picture was taken the first time she went outside. Her name is Poot."

Demi denounced Poot for what it was: more bullying, and an example of how any less-than-flawless photo of a woman is game for ridicule, even viral hatred.

An American Blend

Demi is "proud of my culture and my ethnicity."

Her father was of Mexican descent . . .

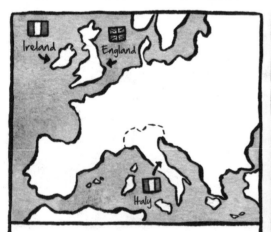

her mother is of Irish, Italian, and English descent.

Also in the blend are American Indian, Portuguese, and Jewish roots.

Wise Big-Sister Words

"Learning to be grateful for our bodies and taking care of them are the best ways for us to empower ourselves physically, mentally, and spiritually."

"Don't let anyone take advantage or manipulate you."
"Put on any song that always makes you feel better."

"Even at your lowest points, keep your sense of humor and use it."

"When you find yourself doubting, stop it right there and say instead, 'I believe in myself.'"

The Gosselins

Turning Real Siblings
into a Reality Show

No matter what the Gosselin children do for the rest of their lives, cameras will be trained on them. Though still very young, they're famous . . . for being famous. Sibling celebrities.

After all, how many families produce eight children within three years?

Said their mother, Kate: "More than anything else in my life, I wanted to be a mom." Her wish was granted many times over.

First up were the twins, Cara and Madelyn (Mady), Cara being the older by six minutes.

When the twins were three, Kate became pregnant with sextuplets—yes, six babies. The pregnancy was so difficult that she had to spend the last two months of it in bed. She described herself as a "blob on bed rest." With Kate resting, taking care of the little twins was a mighty challenge. Her husband, Jon, and others helped. All the Gosselin siblings are biracial, as Jon is second-generation Korean.

The bed rest made the difference, and the six new Gosselins—Alexis, Hannah, Aaden, Collin, Leah, and Joel—were born in 2004 in Hershey, Pennsylvania. A team of more than fifty doctors and nurses were on hand for the unusual delivery. The six babies—all except Collin weighed less than three pounds—were delivered within three minutes of one another.

To leave the hospital, the babies had to gain weight and be able to breathe and swallow without the aid of machines. Over the next two months, they were released from the hospital one or two at a time. Getting them home took the planning and precision of a military maneuver. Because they were already famous, reporters and photographers crowded outside the hospital door to glimpse each new Gosselin.

The first night that all six were safely home, Kate thought they sounded like a herd of goats: "All around us were soft snorty little grunts and snores."

In the middle of the night, she had to wonder, *Who are all of these little people?*

Next up was getting to know them as human beings—and finding out how different they were. Then she had to figure out how to be a hands-on mom to eight children under five years of age.

In one of the bigger adjustments in the history of siblings, Cara and Mady were instant big sisters to six. Suddenly they had to share their mom and dad, their stuff, and the spotlight.

The family's new reality was full of constant babble and chaos as Kate and Jon had to juggle bottle preparation, laundry, and getting the babies to bed. And sleepless nights—the sleep deprivation was extreme.

Predictably, the house always smelled of dirty diapers, a problem that Kate claimed was improved by "the natural intoxicating perfume that newborns exude." It didn't help that Leah had a constant digestive issue that led to projectile vomiting.

All the caretaking was like an especially intricate dance routine. There were thirty-six bottles of various formulas that had to be mixed each morning, with six feedings a day to manage, and some thirty-six diaper changes a day.

In a case of "It takes a village to raise a child," the daily routine included a wide assortment of volunteers. There were relatives, people from church, neighbors—but also looky-loos, people just stopping by to gawk. No sooner would Kate and Jon succeed in changing, feeding, and settling down one baby than it would be the next one's turn. . . .

Jon took sole charge at bath time. Giving six baths and getting six bodies into pj's took a solid hour.

Kate kept everything hyperorganized with lists, including one of who had pooped that day. Making lists was her way of staying sane, though, looking back later, she wished she had spent less time organizing and "more time nibbling little feet and cuddling up."

The first year's count was 13,000 diaper changes and bottle feedings, and a thousand loads of laundry. The babies created so much trash that Jon and Kate had to leave bribes to get the trash collectors to pick it up.

It did help that companies were donating goods, gift cards, groceries, diapers, car seats, and cribs. But the Gosselins were not wealthy and struggled financially.

They also struggled emotionally. Every milestone in child development had to be multiplied by six—six babies shrieking with the pains of teething and, eventually, six babies to potty-train, for example.

As the babies moved to solid food, helpers had to spoon applesauce (luckily, a company had donated a lifetime supply) into one mouth after another. They sat, plopped in front of a Baby Einstein video, at a special six-seat feeding table, mouths open, like a flock of baby birds.

Later, the family bought bread twelve loaves at a time. A typical breakfast used up four boxes of cereal or two dozen eggs every day.

Six toddlers had to be taught the safest way to get down the stairs at the same time: "First, sit on your heinies," Kate would say, "with your feet out in front like this . . . then slowly slide down one step at a time."

The babies matured at different rates. Hannah and Leah were the first to talk and translated the babble of the others.

They all learned to crawl at different times, with Alexis bringing up the rear, content to watch as the others struggled to stay upright. Joel was the fastest at crawling, then lagged behind in walking until he kept getting hit in the head by toys that the walkers were carrying. Later he became the first sextuplet to ride a bike without training wheels.

As they grew, the sextuplets developed distinct personalities. The oldest, Alexis (Lexi), loves making people laugh. She's goofy and outgoing. The loudest Gosselin, she likes to roughhouse with her brothers. Her favorite animal is the alligator, and she wants to work with animals when she grows up.

Hannah (Hannie) seems like the oldest in terms of maturity. She is particular about everything and worries if anyone is sick

or things aren't fair. Her role model is Cara, and her best friend is Leah.

Aaden was the smallest of the sextuplets at birth. He is near-sighted and started wearing glasses at age two. This, combined with his curious and thoughtful personality, led to his nickname, Professor. Within the family, Aaden is notorious for his stinky feet. A bit self-conscious about it, he has been known to check the odor of his feet by smelling them himself.

Collin was the biggest of the brood. As a baby, his head was too big for his body, sometimes causing him to topple over. He remains the biggest sextuplet, eats the most, and finishes his food first. He likes everything to be in a particular order, lining up his shoes perfectly, for example. His closest bond is with Cara, and he's earned a reputation as "Mommy's helper boy."

Leah, also known as the "little princess," excels at luring the rest into trouble. She loves pandas and penguins, and her BFF is Hannah.

Joel, the youngest, seems to be the most easygoing Gosselin,

though he is known to whine when he senses an injustice. He likes to smell things, from food to toys to dogs.

The siblings had to learn to entertain themselves and be more self-reliant than most kids. Kate's favorite activity to keep them all busy was to give each one a pile of shaving cream and tell them they could do anything they wanted with it except put it in their mouth. A well-known sticker company sent boxes of stickers, which provided many happy hours of play.

Cara and Mady proved themselves as outstanding big sisters, assisting in various ways. Cara had a talent for keeping the others under control, like a schoolteacher. Mady loved to help out in the kitchen. Having taught themselves how to read when they were four, the twins took pleasure in teaching their younger siblings.

But sometimes jealousy struck. Mady would get mad and act

out; Cara would look sad. Kate made sure they got extra attention whenever possible, throwing them lavish birthday parties. Their eleventh-birthday celebration included roller skating, pizza, and boys' and girls' slumber parties at a hotel.

"It's not fair!" was probably their most common complaint— but that's the battle cry of siblings everywhere. "Life's not fair" was their parents' only logical response.

The Gosselins presented a whole new wrinkle in the history of siblinghood. Getting the gang prepared to go anywhere was such an ordeal that they spent more time indoors than most kids, socializing only with siblings. "I often tell my children," Kate said, "'Look around; these are, and will always be, your best friends.'"

At first they left the house only for doctor appointments. The family got a little more mobile when they bought the "Big Blue Bus"—a van so large that it had space to fit two adults and eight car seats, plus two triple strollers.

Financial struggles continued, with Jon being out of work, leaving the family dependent on the kindness of others.

A TV station approached them: How would this unique family like to have their lives filmed for TV? Audiences would be awestruck at the spectacle and challenge of raising so many children at once.

Kate and Jon liked the case the station made: "We do television to help people understand other people better."

In 2007, after two successful one-hour specials, the family

got its own regular reality show, *Jon and Kate Plus 8*. The family was filmed three to four days per week and received payment for appearing on the show.

It turned out to be extremely popular, one of the station's highest-rated programs. In part, it was because people liked to see things go wrong. Kate, sleep deprived and coping with so much, became the mom some people loved to hate, picturing themselves more in control, and maybe not putting their kids on TV in the first place.

So the Gosselin siblings grew up in the glare of TV lights permanently installed in their home. Their main job was to look adorable, and they became pros. The kids took to their new life-style well and enjoyed the attention. They loved the crew and gave them nicknames. They would greet Stinky, Meatball, Wave, and the others with hugs, and would play games, ride piggyback, and perform skits for them.

The show was possibly more stressful for the parents. The family lost all their privacy, with people taking pictures through their windows and posting them online.

The stress often showed on camera, and the marriage didn't survive it. By 2009, the couple had announced their separation. While the marriage ended, the show continued, now called *Kate Plus 8*. America has watched the Gosselins grow up, and the family has been open to sharing their triumphs and struggles.

On their sixteenth birthday, Cara told Mady, "You drive me crazy but I'm proud to call you my best friend and sister." Cara wants to become a doctor, while Mady is interested in being a performer.

As they and their siblings grow older, their attitudes may change about how much or how little they want to be exposed on TV. For now, the show goes on, but stay tuned.

Don't Worry

"People expect us to be damaged," said Cara in 2014. Mady explained further: "People think we're supposed to be messed up, like, 'Oooooh, the poor Gosselin kids, they're going to be scarred for life, waaaaah.'"

"Here's the big news: we're not messed up." When the siblings have problems, they get help—all of them have had counseling, and Collin has spent time in a residential program to help with his behavior issues.

New Developments

The Gosselins weren't the first family to experience multiple births, but they were the first to share the experience on TV. In honing ever-more-successful treatments for fertility difficulties, doctors have made multiple births more common.

And the Gosselins have been joined by other families of multiples with their own shows.

The World Record

Kate was far from setting a world record as a mom.

That honor goes to a Russian woman in the 1770s, Valentina Vassilyeva.

Valentina had sixteen pairs of twins, seven sets of triplets, and four sets of quadruplets.

Sources

General

Colt, George Howe. *Brothers*. New York: Scribner, 2012.

Fishel, Elizabeth. *Sisters: Shared Histories, Lifelong Ties*. Berkeley: Conari, 1997.

Hemphill, C. Dallett. *Siblings: Brothers and Sisters in American History*. New York: Oxford University Press, 2011.

Leman, Kevin. *The Birth Order Book: Why You Are the Way You Are*. Grand Rapids: Revell, 2009.

Sulloway, Frank J. *Born to Rebel: Birth Order, Family Dynamics, and Creative Lives*. New York: Pantheon, 1996.

Queens Elizabeth I & Mary I (Bloody Mary)

Buchanan, Jane. *Mary Tudor: Courageous Queen or Bloody Mary?* New York: Franklin Watts, 2008.

Doran, Susan. *Elizabeth I and Her Circle*. Oxford: Oxford University Press, 2015.

englishhistory.net/tudor/monarchs/queen-elizabeth-i

englishhistory.net/tudor/monarchs/queen-mary-1

Erickson, Carolly. *The First Elizabeth*. New York: St. Martin's, 1983.

Guy, John. *The Children of Henry VIII*. Oxford: Oxford University Press, 2013.

Home of the Royal Family, royal.uk

Krull, Kathleen. *Lives of Extraordinary Women: Rulers, Rebels (and What the Neighbors Thought).* New York: Harcourt, 2000.

Maurer, Gretchen. *Mary Tudor: "Bloody Mary."* Foster City, CA: Goosebottom, 2011.

Porter, Linda. *The First Queen of England: The Myth of "Bloody Mary."* New York: St. Martin's, 2007.

Slavicek, Louise Chipley. *Mary I: Bloody Mary.* Farmington Hills, MI: Blackbirch, 2005.

Somerset, Anne. *Elizabeth I.* New York: St. Martin's, 1991.

tudorhistory.org/elizabeth

tudorhistory.org/mary

Chang & Eng Bunker

Collins, David R. *Eng and Chang: The Original Siamese Twins.* New York: Dillon, 1994.

Dreger, Alice Domurat. *One of Us: Conjoined Twins and the Future of Normal.* Cambridge: Harvard University Press, 2004.

Eng and Change Bunker Digital Project, dc.lib.unc.edu/cdm /landingpage/collection/bunkers

Jackson, Donna M. *Twin Tales: The Magic and Mystery of Multiple Birth.* Boston: Little, Brown, 2001.

Mütter Museum, "Cast and Livers of Chang and Eng Bunker," muttermuseum.org/exhibitions/cast-and-livers-of-chang -and-eng-bunker

Orser, Joseph Andrew. *The Lives of Chang and Eng: Siam's Twins in Nineteenth-Century America.* Chapel Hill: University of North Carolina Press, 2014.

Segal, Nancy L. *Entwined Lives: Twins and What They Tell Us About Human Behavior.* New York: Dutton, 1999.

Wu, Cynthia. *Chang and Eng Reconnected: The Original Siamese Twins in American Culture.* Philadelphia: Temple University Press, 2012.

Edwin & John Wilkes Booth

Alford, Terry. *Fortune's Fool: The Life of John Wilkes Booth.* New York: Oxford University Press, 2015.

Giblin, James Cross. *Good Brother, Bad Brother: The Story of Edwin Booth and John Wilkes Booth.* New York: Clarion, 2005.

Swanson, James L. *Manhunt: The 12-Day Chase for Lincoln's Killer.* New York: Morrow, 2006.

Titone, Nora. *My Thoughts Be Bloody: The Bitter Rivalry Between Edwin and John Wilkes Booth That Led to an American Tragedy.* New York: Free Press, 2010.

Vincent & Theo van Gogh

Cernak, Linda. *Vincent van Gogh*. Mankato, MN: The Child's World, 2015.

Greenberg, Jan, and Sandra Jordan. *Vincent van Gogh: Portrait of an Artist*. New York: Delacorte, 2001.

Krull, Kathleen. *Lives of the Artists: Masterpieces, Messes (and What the Neighbors Thought)*. New York: Harcourt, 1995.

Naifeh, Steven, and Gregory White Smith. *Van Gogh: The Life*. New York: Random House, 2011.

Sweetman, David. *Van Gogh: His Life and His Art*. New York: Simon & Schuster, 1990.

Van Gogh, Vincent. *Ever Yours: The Essential Letters*. Edited by Leo Jansen, Hans Luijten, and Nienke Bakker. New Haven: Yale University Press, 2014.

Van Gogh Museum, Amsterdam, vangoghmuseum.nl/en

Vincent van Gogh Gallery, vangoghgallery.com

Whiting, Jim. *Vincent van Gogh*. Hockessin, DE: Mitchell Lane, 2008.

Wilbur & Orville Wright

Collins, Mary. *Airborne: A Photobiography of Wilbur and Orville Wright*. Washington, DC: National Geographic, 2003.

Freedman, Russell. *The Wright Brothers: How They Invented the Airplane*. New York: Holiday House, 1991.

Kelly, Fred C., editor. *Miracle at Kitty Hawk: The Letters of Wilbur and Orville Wright.* New York: Da Capo, 2002.

Maurer, Richard. *The Wright Sister: Katharine Wright and Her Famous Brothers.* Brookfield, CT: Roaring Brook, 2003.

McCullough, David. *The Wright Brothers.* New York: Simon & Schuster, 2015.

The Wright Brothers, wrightbrothers.info

Smithsonian National Air and Space Museum, "The Wright Brothers and the Invention of the Aerial Age," airandspace .si.edu/exhibitions/wright-brothers/online

Walt & Roy Disney

Barrier, Michael. *The Animated Man: A Life of Walt Disney.* Berkeley: University of California Press, 2008.

The Disney Wiki, disney.wikia.com/wiki/The_Disney_Wiki

Gabler, Neal. *Walt Disney: The Triumph of the American Imagination.* New York: Knopf, 2006.

Gitlin, Martin. *Walt Disney: Entertainment Visionary.* Edina, MN: Abdo, 2010.

Mouse Planet, mouseplanet.com

Orr, Tamra B. *Walt Disney: The Man Behind the Magic.* New York: Scholastic, 2014.

Susanin, Timothy S. *Walt Before Mickey: Disney's Early Years,*

1919–1928. Jackson: University Press of Mississippi, 2011.

Thomas, Bob. *Building a Company: Roy O. Disney and the Creation of an Entertainment Empire.* New York: Hyperion, 1998.

"Walt Disney." *American Experience.* PBS, 2015.

Walt Disney Family Museum, waltdisney.com

The Romanovs

Alexander Palace Time Machine, alexanderpalace.org/palace

Brewster, Hugh. *Anastasia's Album: The Last Tsar's Youngest Daughter Tells Her Own Story.* New York: Hyperion, 1996.

Fleming, Candace. *The Family Romanov: Murder, Rebellion & the Fall of Imperial Russia.* New York: Schwartz & Wade, 2014.

Massie, Robert K. *Nicholas and Alexandra: The Classic Account of the Fall of the Romanov Dynasty.* New York: Random House, 2000.

Nicholas and Alexandra: The Last Imperial Family of Tsarist Russia, nicholasandalexandra.com

Prince Michael of Greece. *Nicholas and Alexandra: The Family Albums.* London: Tauris Parke, 1992.

Rappaport, Helen. *The Last Days of the Romanovs: Tragedy at Ekaterinburg.* New York: St. Martin's, 2008.

———. *The Romanov Sisters: The Lost Lives of the Daughters of Nicholas and Alexandra.* New York: St. Martin's, 2014.

Romanov Memorial, "Ipatiev House," romanov-memorial.com

The Royal Martyrs of Russia, serfes.org/royal

Royal Russia, angelfire.com/pa/ImperialRussian

Vyrubova, Anna Aleksandrovna. *The Romanov Family Album.* New York: Vendome Press, 1982.

The Kennedys

The photographers and writers of the *Boston Globe. Ted Kennedy: Scenes from an Epic Life.* New York: Simon & Schuster, 2009.

Clarke, Thurston. *The Last Campaign: Robert F. Kennedy and 82 Days that Inspired America.* New York: Holt, 2008.

Clymer, Adam. *Edward M. Kennedy: A Biography.* New York: Morrow, 1999.

Cooper, Ilene. *Jack: The Early Years of John F. Kennedy.* New York: Dutton, 2003.

Harrison, Barbara, and Daniel Terris. *A Ripple of Hope: The Life of Robert F. Kennedy.* New York: Lodestar Books, 1997.

John F. Kennedy Presidential Library and Museum, jfklibrary.org

Kennedy, Maxwell Taylor, editor. *Make Gentle the Life of This World: The Vision of Robert F. Kennedy.* New York: Broadway, 1999.

Krull, Kathleen. *The Brothers Kennedy: John, Robert, Edward*. New York: Simon & Schuster, 2010.

Larson, Kate Clifford. *Rosemary: The Hidden Kennedy Daughter*. Boston: Houghton Mifflin, 2015.

Mahoney, Richard D. *Sons and Brothers: The Days of Jack and Bobby Kennedy*. New York: Arcade, 1999.

Martin, Harold H. "The Amazing Kennedys." *Saturday Evening Post*, September 7, 1957.

O'Brien, Michael. *John F. Kennedy: A Biography*. New York: St. Martin's, 2005.

Rappaport, Doreen. *Jack's Path of Courage: The Life of John F. Kennedy*. New York: Hyperion, 2010.

Robert F. Kennedy Human Rights Organization, rfkhumanrights.org

Salinger, Pierre, Edwin Guthman, Frank Mankiewicz, and John Seigenthaler, editors. *An Honorable Profession: A Tribute to Robert F. Kennedy*. New York: Doubleday, 1968.

Sommer, Shelley. *John F. Kennedy: His Life and Legacy*. New York: HarperCollins, 2005.

Stabler, David. *Kid Presidents: True Tales of Childhood from America's Presidents*. Philadelphia: Quirk Books, 2014.

Thomas, Evan. *Robert Kennedy: His Life*. New York: Simon & Schuster, 2000.

The Jacksons

Hirshey, Gerri. "Michael Jackson: Life as a Man in the Magical Kingdom." *Rolling Stone,* February 17, 1983.

Jackson, Janet. *True You: A Journey to Loving and Finding Yourself.* New York: Simon & Schuster, 2011.

Jackson, Jermaine. *You Are Not Alone: Michael, Through a Brother's Eyes.* New York: Simon & Schuster, 2011.

Jackson, La Toya. *La Toya: Growing Up in the Jackson Family.* New York: Penguin, 1991.

Jackson, Michael. *Moonwalk.* New York: Crown, 2009.

Manning, Steve. *The Jacksons.* Indianapolis: Bobbs-Merrill, 1976.

The editors of *Rolling Stone. Michael.* New York: HarperCollins, 2009.

Stephen Colbert & His Ten Older Siblings

Apatow, Judd. *Sick in the Head: Conversations About Life and Comedy.* New York: Random House, 2015.

Colbert Nation, cc.com/shows/the-colbert-report

The Late Show with Stephen Colbert, cbs.com/shows/the-late-show-with-stephen-colbert

Rogak, Lisa. *And Nothing but the Truthiness: The Rise (and Further Rise) of Stephen Colbert.* New York: St. Martin's, 2012.

Peyton & Eli Manning

Manning, Archie, and Peyton Manning. *Manning*. New York: HarperCollins, 2000.

Manning Passing Academy, manningpassingacademy.com

Mattern, Joanne. *Peyton Manning: Indianapolis Colts Star Quarterback*. Hockessin, DE: Mitchell Lane, 2007.

Nagle, Jeanne. *Archie, Peyton, and Eli Manning: Football's Royal Family*. New York: Rosen, 2010.

PeyBack Foundation, peytonmanning.com

Peyton Manning, peytonmanning.com

Pro Football Hall of Fame, profootballhof.com

Vacchiano, Ralph. *Eli Manning: The Making of a Quarterback*. New York: Sports Publishing, 2012.

Serena & Venus Williams

Donaldson, Madeline. *Venus and Serena Williams*. Minneapolis: Lerner, 2008.

Edmondson, Jacqueline. *Venus and Serena Williams: A Biography*. Westport, CT: Greenwood Press, 2005.

Watson, Galadriel Findlay. *Venus and Serena Williams*. New York: Weigl Publishers, 2006.

Wertheim, L. Jon. *Venus Envy: A Sensational Season Inside the Women's Tennis Tour*. New York: HarperCollins, 2001.

Williams, Richard, with Bart Davis. *Black and White: The Way I See It.* New York: Simon & Schuster, 2014.

Williams, Serena, with Daniel Paisner. *On the Line.* New York: Grand Central, 2009.

Williams, Venus, and Serena Williams, with Hilary Beard. *Venus and Serena: Serving from the Hip: 10 Rules for Living, Loving, and Winning.* Boston: Houghton Mifflin, 2005.

Venus and Serena Williams Tutorial/Tennis Academy, www .venusserenatennisacademy.org

Venus Williams, venuswilliams.com

Princes William & Harry

Andersen, Christopher. *After Diana: William, Harry, Charles, and the Royal House of Windsor.* New York: Hyperion, 2007.

The Current Royal Family/The British Monarchy, royal.uk

The Duke and Duchess of Cambridge (William and Kate), dukeandduchessofcambridge.org

Hill, Duncan, et al., editors. *The Royal Family: A Year by Year Chronicle of the House of Windsor.* New York: Parragon, 2013.

Junor, Penny. *Prince William: The Man Who Will Be King.* New York: Pegasus Books, 2012.

Nicholl, Katie. *William and Harry: Behind the Palace Walls.* New York: Weinstein, 2010.

Prince Harry of Wales, princehenryofwales.org

The Royal Foundation of the Duke and Duchess of Cambridge and Prince Harry, royalfoundation.com

Demi Lovato & Madison De La Garza

Blumm, K. C. "Demi Lovato Is a Protective Big Sister Says Madison De La Garza." *People,* August 14, 2015.

De La Garza, Madison. Letter in *Latina Magazine,* September 2015.

Demi Lovato, demilovato.com

Lovato, Demi. *Staying Strong: 365 Days a Year.* New York: Feiwel and Friends, 2013.

Meinking, Mary. *Demi Lovato.* North Mankato, MN: Capstone, 2013.

Morreale, Marie. "*Camp Rock:* Demi Lovato." *Scholastic News,* June 16, 2008.

Peppas, Lynn. *Demi Lovato.* New York: Crabtree, 2013.

Shaffer, Jody Jensen. *Demi Lovato: Taking Another Chance.* Minneapolis: Lerner, 2014.

Tracy, Kathleen. *Demi Lovato.* Hockessin, DE: Mitchell Lane, 2010.

The Gosselins

Gosselin, Jon, Kate Gosselin, and Beth Carson. *Multiple Blessings: Surviving to Thriving with Twins and Sextuplets.* Grand Rapids: Zondervan, 2008.

Gosselin, Kate. *Eight Little Faces: A Mom's Journey.* Grand Rapids: Zondervan, 2009.

———. *I Just Want You to Know: Letters to My Kids on Love, Faith, and Family.* Grand Rapids: Zondervan, 2010.

Jon and Kate Plus 8, tvguide.com/tvshows/jon-kate-plus-8/287169

Kate Plus 8, tlc.com/tv-shows/kate-plus-8

Kate Plus My 8, kateplusmy8.com

Index

About the Author

KATHLEEN KRULL is an award-winning author of a number of highly praised nonfiction books for children, including *The Boy Who Invented TV* and the Lives Of series. She lives in San Diego. For more, visit her on Facebook or at kathleenkrull.com.

About the Illustrator

MAPLE LAM is a children's book author and illustrator. She is an avid history fan and loves graphic novels and comics. She lives in Southern California. For more, visit her at maplelam.com.